OP

Nutrition Careers

OPPORTUNITIES

in

Nutrition
Careers

REVISED EDITION

Carol Coles Caldwell

McGraw-Hill

New York   Chicago   San Francisco   Lisbon   London   Madrid   Mexico City
Milan   New Delhi   San Juan   Seoul   Singapore   Sydney   Toronto

Library of Congress Cataloging-in-Publication Data

Caldwell, Carol C. (Carol Coles)
      Opportunities in nutrition careers / Carol Coles Caldwell. — Rev. ed.
         p.   cm.
      ISBN 0-07-143846-7
      1. Dietetics—Vocational guidance.   I. Title.

   RM218.5.C35   2005
   613.2′023—dc22   2004025052

2 3 4 5 6 7 8 9 0   DOC/DOC   0 9 8 7 6 5

ISBN 0-07-143846-7

Interior design by Rattray Design

McGraw-Hill books are available at special quantity discounts to use as premiums and sales promotions, or for use in corporate training programs. For more information, please write to the Director of Special Sales, Professional Publishing, McGraw-Hill, Two Penn Plaza, New York, NY 10121-2298. Or contact your local bookstore.

This book is printed on acid-free paper.

Contents

Director of nutrition, diet, and fitness. Nutritionist/ writer. Manager, nutrition technical services. Technical information specialist. Nutrition research specialist. Conclusion.

Preface

Nutritionists, of course, have always known that good dietary habits are key to good health. The old adage "You are what you eat" is familiar to everyone, but in recent decades, the public has begun to take those words very seriously, realizing that the body (and the mind) is only as good as the food that fuels it.

As interest in good nutrition and diet increased, so did the number of specialties and subspecialties within this field. But a sound, healthy diet for one person may have little benefit for another. It all depends on an individual's health, cultural background, eating habits, environment, and so forth. Only a professional in nutrition can assemble and interpret all the dieting and health data about an individual and create a reasonable and healthful meal plan for him or her.

Opportunities in Nutrition Careers defines nutrition, explains and explores the various roles of dietitians, and provides information on salaries and job satisfaction. It is an excellent primer to this rapidly growing, exciting field.

Introduction

Both the dietitian and the nutritionist are concerned with providing nutrition-related services to people. The dietitian is considered a health care professional who has credentials as a registered dietitian and who therefore can affect the nutritional care of individuals and groups in health and illness. A nutritionist may have the credentials of a dietitian, or he or she may have acquired the knowledge and experience in nutrition following another path.

The work of the dietitian and the nutritionist includes the application of the science and art of human nutrition in helping people select and obtain food for the primary purpose of nourishing their bodies in health or disease throughout their lives. The professional's participation may include client nutritional assessment and intervention, nutrition education, consultation to food service and management, corporate health promotion, research, and food product/recipe development.

Nutrition as Science and Art

To understand the scope of the profession, it is important to define the terms *nutrition* and *nutritional care*. These are terms that help to describe how a dietitian may choose to practice in various areas.

Nutrition is defined today as the science of food, the nutrients and other substances therein, their action, interaction, and balance in relation to health and disease; and the process by which humans ingest, digest, absorb, transport, utilize, and excrete food substances. In addition, nutrition must be concerned with social, economic, cultural, and psychological implications of food and eating.

Nutritional care is the application of the science of nutrition. It is the art of helping people select and obtain food for the primary purpose of nourishing their bodies. It is essential both in health and disease throughout the life cycle.

The goals of nutritional care are comprehensive. They include improvement of the quality of life, prevention of disease, and clinical therapy during illness. To meet the goals of nutritional care, dietitians practice in many different settings: hospitals or other health care facilities; schools and universities; business and industry food-service operations including restaurants, food chains, airlines, and spas; and community agencies. Dietetic practitioners can be involved in clinical practice, research, management of food-service systems, food processing, cooking, communications (television, radio, newspapers, magazines, computers, public relations, and so forth), and teaching. Whether nutritional care is provided to improve the lives of individuals, manage a large-scale food operation, teach other health scientists and consumers, or explain the nutritive content of food to children, the dietitian will be participating in many sophisticated and multifaceted roles.

The Expanding Role of Nutrition

The role of nutritionists and dietitians in our society is in a state of rapid growth and change. Only a few short years ago, the most basic principles of nutrition were largely unknown to the general public. Today, knowledge of the role of nutrition in human health increasingly is the subject of magazine and newspaper articles, books, television shows, and programs at public meetings. Movie stars, presidents, and other public personalities mention their health and fitness activities. Athletes are quoted on how they maintain their diets and nutritional well-being.

Interest in nutrition is depicted in food product commercials and in newspaper and magazine advertising. Demand for nutritional information on packaged food products has created a new policy, and product labels are increasingly specific about the nutritional value of the products. Hospitals, doctors, and nurses are greatly concerned about nutrition, and many have returned to medical school for the latest information on nutrition and dietetics.

Nutrition courses in public schools, colleges, medical schools, and other educational institutions are on the rise. The result of all this growth has been a flurry of new, widely varied, exciting courses available to the public and to the nutrition specialist.

The Professional Outlook

To the person who is considering a career as a dietitian, a nutritionist, a teacher, a writer, a consultant, a nutrition therapist, or any of a number of new specialties in this area, this is a time of increasingly new opportunities. As the nutrition field grows in the next decade, more and more positions will open up. For some, this period of growth and change will actually mean pioneering in areas of human nutritional care that have not even been imagined today. Just as the health spa is no longer the privilege of only a few, good nutritional practices are no longer within the reach of only the privileged. The public is growing more and more aware of the opportunities for better health and longer life through the use of good nutritional practices—and the demand for professionals in this field will continue to expand along with this public awareness.

1

AN EXCITING AND
CHALLENGING PROFESSION

IT IS A wonderful time to be a dietitian and a nutritional professional. Never before have so many people been so visibly interested
in nutrition. Popular interest in this subject can be measured by the
large number of bestselling diet books, as well as the fortunes being
made by those who serve the public's desire for nutritional information and diet counseling, for health books, and for diet
supplements.

It is now apparent that optimal nutrition can be a strong factor
in maintaining health and preventing disease. Physicians and other
health professionals—as well as corporate presidents, chefs, and
major food-service operators—recognize the value of nutrition. The
complexities of modern medicine demand high-quality nutritional
care, and the general public demands nutritional food and access
to easily understood nutrition information.

A Changing Field

Dramatic changes are occurring in the nutrition profession. These changes are the result of three new developments: (1) computer applications in the nutrition field; (2) the desire of the general population and corporations to know more about nutrition; and (3) the demand by "baby boomers" for more medical education and intervention.[1] The success of this field's expansion relies on the dietitian's ability to provide quality services to the public, at a time when the public is searching for accurate nutritional information and cost-effective health care. Intervention efforts include cultivating healthy nutrition behaviors, identifying appealing modes of exercise, and using varied therapies for nutrition management. A challenge for dietetic professionals is to teach proper, balanced nutrition and motivate individuals to make changes in their lifestyles.

Mapping out a satisfying and successful career path can be one of the biggest challenges facing dietitians today, especially considering the vast array of opportunities presented by a health care environment that is continually evolving. It is essential to choose a career path that you find enjoyable and rewarding; something you are good at and that gives you satisfaction.

Dietitians may act as consultants to small community hospitals, long-term nursing care institutions, or special interest groups such as sports trainers. In industry they may be members of a product development or market research team, or they may be in the sales force. In public health they may supervise nutritional programs for the elderly or for patients recently released from acute-care facilities. In food service they may work with a chef to develop healthy recipes, and in private practice they may develop a marketing plan to identify the need for nutrition services. In the community the dietitian may provide nutritional support or outpatient and in-home counseling services.

Gaining Insight

Before entering this job market, it is critical to determine your individual interests. Dietitians in different types of settings have different types of experiences. Therefore, you should consider what kind of experience you want before searching for a position. Consult the phone directory in your area for nutritionist listings. Call one and ask to set up an interview. Also, ask to shadow the dietitian or nutrition professional for a period of time. This way you will quickly gain an insight into the profession. Ask for information regarding a state affiliate meeting. (See Appendix A for a list of state ADA associations.) This will give you an opportunity to network with and meet dietitians throughout your state. Finally, attend the American Dietetics Association national convention held annually in October.

Career Advancement

No matter what nutrition career path you choose, the key to achieving professional career goals is to avoid common mistakes many registered dietitians make during the job-hunting process.

1. Do not focus on job title alone. Focus more on the details of the job description: required skills, duties, responsibilities of the position, and pay.
2. Do not forget to examine the alternate and/or substitute requirements included in the job posting that meet

minimum requirements. Dietetics professionals are qualified for many different types of positions using their transferable education, training, skills, and experience.

3. Always have your résumé current, as many job opportunities require fast responses.

4. Do not forget that successful leaders stand on principle, not on politics. In other words, be honest and have integrity when representing yourself to a potential employer.

5. When utilizing friends and colleagues as sources for possible job leads, encourage them to be honest with you so they will feel comfortable sharing real thoughts, concerns, and suggestions.

6. Develop a personal transition plan, complete with timelines, actions, and benchmarks to illustrate goals for retooling your knowledge, skills, and experience.

7. Challenge yourself to expand your professional "basket" of skills. Valuable skills include learning how to manage financial budgets, successfully supervising people, and improving public speaking abilities.

8. Do not make a career change without doing your research first. Shadow an expert in the field and/or volunteer your time until you understand your potential new career.

9. Remember to give yourself permission to change your mind. View your job explorations as a professional adventure rather than a personal failure.[2]

10. Making the right decision takes time: time for the challenges associated with breaking into a specialty market to surface, and time to attend to those challenges and make adjustments to create success.

Conclusion

The challenges the nutrition professional faces are exciting. It is a time when nutrition experts can create the world in which they work, but it will take initiative, advanced knowledge, and the development of individual expertise. You will find it a privilege to play a crucial role in this field. Nutrition is an essential component, not only of health and health care, but of life itself.

2

THE DIETITIAN'S HERITAGE

THE PROFESSION OF dietetics, as it is known today, began with the founding of the American Dietetic Association in 1917, under the direction of Lenna Frances Cooper. She believed that there was a need for a conference to formulate a plan for dietetic communication. The first challenge faced by this new organization was how dietitians could best serve the nation's needs during World War I, both at home and overseas.

Administration and Management

Originally, administrative dietetics and food management were the specialties of the profession. The term *dietitian* was associated with those who worked in hospitals. Their objective was to provide quantity food production without loss of quality and to standardize institutional feeding.

Development of Standards

During the 1920s and '30s, the dietitian was involved with support of government regulation and welfare agencies, food labeling, development of labor standards for commercial food service, and development of hospital food-service plans. This dietetic movement was described as "one of the greatest existing forces in the promotion of health and the prevention of disease,"[1] but real advances would be achieved only when the results of nutritional research could be integrated into the practices of the population.

By the 1940s, it had become clear that the profession needed to further develop standards in monitoring the quality of food and to become involved in research to develop new food products. In addition, dietitians were involved in government efforts to develop nutritional standards for the school lunch programs.

Public Information

During the 1950s, the American Dietetic Association began a formal public relations program to promote better understanding and recognition of dietitians' expertise. Dietitians were also urged to contribute to national health, research, and education. They were no longer involved in only food service and quality control but were expanding into all areas that nutrition could affect. These areas included government agencies, food industries, universities and schools, and public health education.

New Methods, Education, and Research

The next decade was a time for dietitians to seek new methods and adapt to changing conditions, a challenge that carried into each subsequent decade as dietitians continued to search for new information and improve the quality of life through nutrition.

In the 1970s, there was increasing participation in education and research. This decade saw the organization of dietetics into four major areas of practice: diet therapy, education, community nutrition, and administration. Interest in legislation also became important as the profession recognized the need for licensing of the dietetic practitioner.

Evaluation and Change

The 1980s were a time of critical evaluation and change. The need for change brought about the emergence of specialties among nutrition professionals. Because of this, twenty-three dietetic practice groups were established, each with its own standing rules, officers, newsletters, goals, and budget. As of 2004–05, the American Dietetic Association has twenty-nine current practice groups.

These practice groups provide American Dietetic Association members who have common interests and skills with a chance to share ideas and expand their expertise. They are:

Clinical Nutrition Management
Consultant Dietitians in Health Care Facilities
Diabetes Care and Education
Dietetic Educators of Practitioners
Dietetic Technicians in Practice
Dietetics in Developmental and Psychiatric Disorders
Dietetics in Physical Medicine and Rehabilitation
Dietitians in Business and Communications
Dietitians in General Clinical Practice
Dietitians in Nutrition Support

Food and Culinary Professionals
Gerontological Nutritionists
HIV/AIDS
Hunger and Environmental Nutrition
Management in Food and Nutrition Systems
Nutrition in Complementary Care
Nutrition Education for the Public
Nutrition Educators of Health Professionals
Nutrition Entrepreneurs
Oncology Nutrition
Pediatric Nutrition
Public Health/Community Nutrition
Renal Dietitians
Research
School Nutrition Services
Sports, Cardiovascular, and Wellness Nutritionists
Vegetarian Nutrition
Weight Management
Women's Health and Reproductive Nutrition

Maintenance of Health

In the 1990s, nutritionists focused on the maintenance of general health versus just the treatment of disease. The objective was to help individuals and groups obtain high-quality, tasty food and develop positive behaviors that maintain and support health as well as meet the demand for nutrition services needed in business and industry.

The American Dietetic Association, along with the practice of dietetics, has expanded into all areas—new food development and preparation, weight management, the treatment and prevention of disease, research, nutrition for sports, and many others. Because of this dynamic growth, there are almost unlimited opportunities in the field of nutrition.

The Twenty-First Century

Now, in the twenty-first century, new influences will emerge creating more opportunities and challenges. These new opportunities for the dietetics profession over the next decade are coming from several broad factors, including:

- Increased need for health counseling
- Interest in diet and nutrition from the public, including food safety
- Increased use of functional foods to prevent illness
- Increasing cultural and ethnic diversity
- The obesity epidemic
- Child nutrition
- Use of the Internet for client communications, learning, and promotion
- Emerging interrelationships among genetics, biotechnology, nutrition, environment, and health[2]

Under these influences, dietitians have the opportunity to transform their field into a cutting-edge profession that addresses emerging and evolving needs of a global society. The time for the nutrition professional is now!

3

CLINICAL DIETETICS AND SUBSPECIALTIES

THIS CHAPTER EXAMINES where clinical dietitians work and what they do on the job. Several subspecialties are highlighted as well.

Clinical Dietetics: A Starting Point

The clinical dietitian is defined as a health care professional who has credentials as a registered dietitian and who affects the nutrition care of individuals and groups in health and illness. The clinical dietitian provides nutrition assessment and planning, implementation, and evaluation services; consults about food-service systems; and manages departmental and personnel functions for nutrition care services. Clinical dietitians also coordinate patient care as a member of the health care team, maintain and update their individual skill and knowledge, and conduct applied research. They may also coordinate and supervise activities of dietetic technicians, both registered and students.

Practice Environments

The clinical dietitian may practice in three professional environments. These include acute care/inpatient, ambulatory care, and long-term care. The acute care/inpatient dietitian may practice as a dietetic technician, clinical; a clinical dietitian; a clinical dietitian, specialist; a pediatric/neonatal dietitian; or as a nutrition support dietitian. In ambulatory care, the positions may include outpatient dietitian, general; outpatient dietitian, specialist; or home-care dietitian. In long-term care, the positions include clinical dietitian, long-term care; and dietetic technician, long-term care.

The long-term care clinical dietitian responsibilities may include:

- Developing and implementing nutrition care plans for residents
- Documenting progress and recommendations
- Providing nutrition education for residents, families, and staff
- Consulting with food-service staff on food preparation, service, and delivery
- Providing services as a consultant to more than one facility or being employed by a single facility

Entry-Level Clinical Dietitian

An entry-level position is defined as one that can be filled by a practitioner with experience of three or fewer years. The following provides information about the skills necessary to perform as an entry-level clinical dietitian. According to the American Dietetic Association, the following responsibilities are those the entry-level clinical dietitian will be able to perform:

I. Plan and organize

A. Use institutional and departmental standards to establish goals and priorities related to clinical nutrition, quality food, ethics, and education

B. Participate in departmental program development using appropriate resources
   1. Compare budget and accounting systems to institutional standards
   2. Plan for computer utilization
   3. Develop guidelines for work schedules
   4. Develop policies and procedures
   5. Review evaluation strategies
   6. Assist with quality assurance planning

C. Formulate an education plan
   1. Plan for personnel training
   2. Plan for nutritional and therapeutic needs of individuals and groups
   3. Select principles and theories of education appropriate for the desired plan

II. Gather and evaluate data

A. Assess nutritional needs of individuals and groups
   1. Collect appropriate information for menu planning
   2. Collect appropriate information on the patient through the use of the medical record; questionnaires; interview; community agencies; anthropometric measurements; intakes of food, nutrients, and fluids; and use of drugs
   3. Establish methods for client inquiry (i.e., client or family interviews to obtain information in relation to physical, emotional, environmental, economic, and cultural factors)

B. Perform accurate dietary calculations and evaluate appropriate application

C. Demonstrate research techniques
   1. Review current literature
   2. Use resource materials effectively
   3. Identify problems, issues, and priorities
   4. Select methodology for study
   5. Implement methodology
   6. Gather and evaluate data for use in improvement of program, system, or procedures

D. Appraise potential of individual for employment and upward mobility based on application and interview

E. Appraise employee for upward mobility based on performance evaluation

F. Evaluate products in relation to availability, cost, quality, and procurement

G. Evaluate nutritional programs and services of private or tax-supported agencies

H. Evaluate outcomes of patient education plan by assessing changes in food habits, teaching methods, and learner achievement

I. Contribute to and retrieve information from computer data storage

III. *Communicate and report*

A. Delegate responsibility to personnel in nutrition care and food-service systems

B. Communicate through verbal and nonverbal means in interviewing, counseling, and evaluating

C. Communicate in writing clearly, concisely, and in understandable terminology

D. Communicate professional expertise in classes, meetings, conferences, and rounds

E. Establish inter- and intradepartmental communication systems

F. Conduct personnel training programs

G. Develop, update, and interpret policies and procedures

H. Monitor personnel utilization by evaluating workload of personnel and approving work schedules

IV. *Counsel and supervise—apply principles of psychology, principles of management, and counseling skills in the supervision and motivation of personnel and clients*

A. Identify problem areas with personnel/clients

B. Assist personnel and clients to identify alternative solutions and implement changes

C. Review progress with personnel and clients

V. *Apply scientific principles—food-service systems management*

A. Establish standards for menu planning to coordinate with production and service

1. Approve regular and modified diet menus for nutrient adequacy, accuracy, and quality appropriate to individuals or groups

2. Evaluate menu cycle for changes

B. Monitor safety, security, and sanitation standards

C. Maintain budget controls

VI. *Apply scientific principles—clinical nutrition*

A. Apply principles of management and nutrition to provide nutritional care for clients

1. Direct and evaluate personnel in the provision of nutritional care

2. Modify expenditures to comply with budget

3. Assess nutritional status and devise an individualized nutrition care plan

4. Implement plan through supervision of patient care and provision of nutrition education and follow-up to client and family

5. Evaluate and revise plan as necessary

B. Translate dietary modifications into menus

1. Evaluate client acceptance of food

2. Evaluate food quality, nutritional adequacy, and accuracy of dietary modification

3. Approve regular and modified diet menus for nutrient adequacy, accuracy, and quality appropriate to individuals

4. Evaluate dietary products and supplements

C. Monitor safety, security, and sanitation standards

D. Determine criteria for disease entities

1. Document nutritional care of client according to established criteria

2. Approve written documentation by dietetic technician

3. Conduct audits of medical records at designated intervals

E. Utilize data for computer-assisted systems

1. Plan menu and evaluate nutrient content

2. Calculate client nutrient intake and utilization

3. Maintain client medical database

4. Prepare criteria for audit

F. Apply current nutrition research for improvement of program or system

VII. *Apply scientific principles in community nutrition—apply principles of management and nutrition to provide nutritional care for clients in a program or agency*

A. Identify nutrition needs in the community

B. Assess community resources

VIII. Demonstrate creativity
  A. Apply creative and innovative methods and ideas
    1. Solve problems
    2. Merchandise products, services, nutrition, and the profession
    3. Plan nutrition and food-service programs
    4. Develop educational methods and teaching aids
  B. Apply scientific principles using innovative methods in food-service management, clinical nutrition, and community nutrition
  C. Continue to seek new ways of communicating with others
IX. Exhibit professional performance and accountability
  A. Maintain registration as a professional dietitian
  B. Practice American Dietetic Association Code of Professional Practice and Guidelines for Professional Conduct
  C. Maintain a professional standard of practice
  D. Maintain current professional knowledge by reviewing the literature, maintaining updated resource files, participating in institutional and professional conferences and seminars, and writing technical reports, critical reviews, and articles
  E. Utilize problem-solving methods
  F. Practice self-assessment and assessment of others by developing goals for improvement
  G. Integrate self into the professional role by applying interpersonal skills and assuming leadership roles in the profession
  H. Integrate own position and role into a program or system
  I. Promote departmental and program objectives
  J. Provide continuing education for staff and personal development based on needs
  K. Determine legal implications in the practice of dietetics and seek appropriate liability coverage
  L. Follow institutional policies for the protection of personnel and clients
  M. Seek information on current legislation affecting personnel, patient care, and the profession
  N. Comply with employer and institutional contracts, and government regulations

These skills represent performance at an entry-level, showing depth of knowledge acquired, but they do not indicate that all practitioners will utilize all skills.

Conclusion

Powerful forces and trends shape the dietetics profession. Under these influences, dietitians have the opportunity to transform their field; to shape their destiny individually. In any chosen profession there is a need to "pay one's dues" so to speak. Employers often prefer the individual who will fit in and be "trained" through the work experience gained within the actual job and not by education alone. Clinical dietetics provides this beginning foundation. Future career development is an open door. What the clinical dietitian chooses to experience and explore is as diverse as the opportunities presented in the following chapters.

Subspecialties

The field of dietetics is becoming very specialized, as is the case in the field of medicine, where physicians often choose to specialize in one area. The clinical dietitian today is expanding her or his skills in the development of a specialty, and many are becoming nutrition experts in highly developed areas.

In this section we will discuss the various segments of clinical dietetics: research, pediatrics, critical care, renal dietetics, and diabetes. These subspecialties broaden the scope of clinical dietetic practice and provide interested individuals an opportunity to become expert in a particular area.

Research Specialist

Dietitians become specialized in the area of research through their work in clinical research centers and through public health projects. Most start out in general clinical practice and then go on to research, for which a master's degree in science is usually required. The research environment may be in a university, a hospital (inpatient and/or outpatient setting), or a public health setting.

Candidates interested in research work need to be careful, objective, and self-starters with clinical experience. Additional training may include the areas of grant writing to acquire money, scientific journal writing, and statistics.

Positive aspects of choosing a career in this area include the ability to work independently and with other high-level professionals. Activity in research also demands the development of knowledge of many aspects of nutrition, for example, biochemical, physiological, and psychological. With substantial research training and experience, a registered dietitian can move from one area to another to do research, rather than staying in one specialization area.

The future direction of research will probably focus on the effectiveness of nutritional intervention, as society realizes the importance of preventive measures in terms of both cost and health effectiveness. Although the exact nature of the link between nutrition factors and health remains controversial, there appears to be a broad consensus that diet, nutrition, and eating habits are significantly related to health status. These health issues will expand the opportunities available to the research dietitian.

Pediatrics Specialist

Dietitians enter pediatric practice for the opportunity to work with children. Becoming specialized in pediatrics requires practice in a children's hospital or a hospital with a pediatric unit, or may require an advanced degree specializing in infant/child nutrition. Work settings vary, but usually the practitioner begins in a general hospital pediatric environment and then moves on to do other pediatric work. These environments may include medical centers, hospitals, schools, day-care centers, physician offices, and research centers.

Training for entry-level positions in pediatric practice includes registration with one to two years of experience in the subspecialty area.

The demand for pediatric practitioners will be influenced by the birth rate, expanding child-care programs, legislative trends, and technology. Another area that will impact pediatric practice will be the expanded focus on maternal nutrition to improve the outcome of pregnancy. This area may extend the pediatric practitioner's involvement to include maternal and prenatal care as well as neonatal intensive care units.

Critical-Care Specialist

Dietitians in critical care have a strong therapeutic background, typically working in a university or teaching hospital providing care to the critically ill patient. Most have obtained a master's degree or advanced training beyond the clinical internship. Positive features of this specialty include increased contact with medical staff and opportunities for research, teaching, and publishing.

Critical-care dietitians work with parenteral and enteral nutrition, nutritional assessments, and drug-nutrient interactions. They also work closely with patients to improve nutritional status.

Subspecialties in this area are increasing due to the importance of nutrition in critical illness and the specifics of nutrition therapy. These subspecialties include nutrition support services, oncology, hematology, neonatology, and advanced-burn care.

These specialties involve high-pressure work environments and long hours that demand leadership, assertiveness, and career commitment from the dietetic professional.

Renal Specialist

Renal dietetics deals with nutrition therapy for those individuals with kidney problems. Training for this specialty area requires clinical experience with advanced training, usually on a renal unit in a hospital or dialysis center.

Registered dietitians interested in practicing in this area require special traits to handle intense, long-term patient care, including the patients' psychological and sociological needs. They must be dedicated and have an interest in maintaining current educational status. Rapid changes in knowledge in this area necessitate constant continuing education.

Major work activities of renal dietitians include patient and family education, development of teaching materials, participation in medical rounds, interpretation of laboratory tests, and nutrition education of allied professionals. These responsibilities require knowledge about food composition, drug-nutrient interaction, and fluid electrolyte management in the body.

Diabetes Specialist

Dietitians specializing in diabetes care and education usually work in outpatient facilities or inpatient programs provided by hospitals. The required education includes a bachelor's degree in science with registration status. Additional coursework or a master's degree is not required but is helpful due to the complexity of the disease.

Diabetes care requires long-term treatment and patient education. This provides the dietitian with an opportunity to develop individualized long-term care and to follow the patient and family for an extended time. The dietitian will develop nutrition care plans and educate the client regarding nutrition, psychosocial problems, and exercise. Diabetes care also enables the dietitian to work as a team member.

Opportunities in this area will probably expand due to the growing incidence and increasing knowledge of the disease. Also, technology will continue to shape this area of practice, as research and computers further affect methods of treatment.

Conclusion

Many of these clinical subspecialties require advanced training after registration, which includes a master's degree or Ph.D. in science, and significant work experience within the specialty area. This trend will continue as research and technology expand the "science" of dietetics and nutrition. Also, dietitians will do more independent research, develop policies and procedures, and consult and teach individuals and groups.

4

COMMUNITY DIETETICS

THE DIETITIAN IN a community setting plays an important role as a member of the health care team. The community dietitian counsels individuals and groups on nutritional practices designed to prevent disease and promote good health. Working in public health clinics, home health agencies, and health maintenance organizations, they evaluate individual needs, develop nutritional care plans, and instruct individuals and their families. Dietitians working in home health agencies may provide instruction on grocery shopping and food preparation to the elderly, or to patients with AIDS, cancer, or diabetes.

Home Health Care

The community dietitian will often provide nutrition services to clients in their homes. Usually a referral is made from a hospital health team to the dietitian. The dietitian reviews the patient's medical record, takes a dietary history, assesses the patient's nutritional status, records food likes and dislikes, and develops a nutritional care plan based on pertinent information. The nutrition care plan will then help determine what services the dietitian will provide. These services may include assessment of dietary intake by computer nutrient analysis; consultation with physicians prescribing diets; client and family counseling; follow-up conferences and in-service education with nurses, therapists, and home health aides; and the recording, reporting, and monitoring of the progress and results of nutritional care.

Once developed, the plan is then discussed with the client or home sponsor for the client. Issues that could arise in relation to home care include weight gain from overeating, lack of exercise, and complications in medical conditions. It is important to maintain contact with other health team members, and the community dietitian may need to expand the care plan as the case proceeds.

The dietitian, by maintaining contact with the other health care providers, can identify specific problems and refer them to the team member responsible for that area of specialization. In addition, "mini" home nutrition courses that focus on different areas of nutrition can be provided. The dietitian may provide sample menus for normal and modified diets, depending on the client's lifestyle and medical therapy. The dietitian needs to be aware of food costs, who purchases the food, cultural food preferences, and available food preparation facilities. In this way, home visits provide an opportunity for the dietitian to identify socioeconomic problems and determine instructional techniques to use in gaining acceptance and adherence to the diet and nutrition care plan.

Although not all clients need nutrition services provided in the home, many clients do need the assistance of a dietitian, including:

1. Those whose diets need modification
2. Those whose conditions don't improve because of an improper diet
3. Those whose food plans are prescribed as part of the overall treatment of their conditions
4. Those who need to be monitored, i.e., malnourished or undernourished patients
5. Those who need dietary counseling but are unable to travel
6. Those who need follow-up after discharge from a hospital/nursing home

Professional Benefits

The professional benefits of providing home health care nutrition services are many. Home health care provides the ability to develop a long-term care plan for the client and to provide continued follow-up. The dietitian performs both independently and as a team member, and he or she is responsible for the development of educational materials for client use.

In addition, the dietitian, by providing home health services, may reduce the total cost of health care. Examples of potential cost savings are:

1. Reducing need for re-hospitalization because of malnutrition, uncontrolled diabetes, and other conditions
2. Preventing fractures due to disorientation or weakness related to malnutrition
3. Delaying kidney dialysis treatment
4. Preventing food poisoning from improper food sanitation at home

5. Permitting earlier discharge of patients with parenteral or enteral feedings
6. Assisting the patient to understand and use new technologies, thus preventing or delaying re-institutionalization
7. Hastening healing of postoperative patients
8. Using a trained professional who is more efficient and accurate in the adjustment and readjustment of individualized diets

Educational requirements include entry-level status and two to three years of experience in a clinical setting. An advanced degree (M.S.) is preferred.

Health Maintenance Organizations

Health maintenance organizations (HMOs) are comprehensive medical facilities where, through an employer, families and/or individuals prepay for health care. HMOs were developed to restructure health care delivery systems to provide equitable, high-quality care for all; provide optimal utilization of health personnel; control costs; and satisfy consumers. They are designed to provide health services to individuals and families for a fixed premium paid in advance by subscribers. An HMO is dedicated to providing comprehensive care, defined as a full range of health services with emphasis on prevention; care continuity, coordinated on a family basis, throughout each member's life cycle and health-sickness cycle; and care that is organized and carried out to give maximum health care service for the consumer dollars.

The basic principle by which HMO operations will be successful lies in keeping people well, to avoid the more complex and costly services needed to treat illness and return people to health. In this way, the HMO provides a medical setting outside the hospital where a dietitian can develop a varied practice and become more involved with each client by providing follow-up care.

Professional Roles

Dietitians in this area are diet counselors, health educators, and program evaluators. The dietitian deals with both individuals and families, as well as with the health care team, to provide total health services. In the role of diet counselor, the dietitian provides diet therapy to diabetics, cardiovascular patients, and patients with hypertension, and diet therapy during and following pregnancy. As the health educator, the dietitian teaches self-care, using nutrition as a framework to build positive behavior patterns. The dietitian may also be involved in specialty clinics to deal with obesity, alcoholism, smoking cessation, and weight reduction. As a program evaluator, the dietitian has the opportunity to work with HMO administrators to initiate new and evaluate ongoing programs.

Nutrition Services

Nutrition services in an HMO, as suggested by the American Dietetic Association, may be as follows:

Health appraisal and referral

To identify potential problems and plan for continuing surveillance or appropriate care

- Assessment of food practices and nutritional status
- Referral for corroboration
- Data input into patient information systems

Environmental protection and disease prevention; health maintenance

To prepare patients and their families to assume responsibility for their own care and to manage their early symptoms to prevent complications

- Individual counseling
- Group teaching
- Development and/or evaluation of nutrition methods and materials
- Training and continuing education for medical, dental, and other professional staff; technical consultation
- Training and continuing education for dietetic supportive personnel
- Referral to, and liaison with, food assistance and other nutrition-related community programs
- Leadership in seeking solutions to community-wide nutrition problems
- Consultation provided to group-care facilities

Acute and intensive care

To develop and implement immediate and long-range individualized nutritional care plans for in- or outpatients

- Most of the activities described above
- Ongoing participation in health team planning, direct nutritional assessment and counseling, and evaluation
- Planning appropriate group food service
- Health team staff conferences

- Initial and follow-up counseling in regard to normal and therapeutic nutritional needs
- Input into clinical records
- Restoration and extended care

Long-term care

To assist patients and their families with long-term health problems and to attain and maintain adequate diets

- Most of the activities described above
- Assistance in adjusting home environment to maximize independent functioning in activities in and outside the home
- Liaison with noncontact services or programs helpful in carrying out the nutritional care plan[1]

Nutritional care activities clearly will overlap and seldom will be restricted to a single phase of operation.

Education

The education required of the dietitian is a baccalaureate degree with registration credentials; a master's degree is suggested. The additional training in research and analysis that a master's degree includes will give the dietitian more credibility and an increased opportunity for input into planning programs at the HMO.

Also helpful is knowledge of and experience in community organization and community health services and resources to provide counseling and direction in planning and implementing nutritional care. The dietitian should be capable of training and supervising dietetic personnel and coordinating nutrition programs with other health care services.

Job satisfaction in this area is high because dietitians are occupying positions where they are gaining respect, credibility, and public confidence.

Conclusion

Community dietitians increasingly will be challenged to demonstrate specialized competencies and meet the total needs of the community. As a health team member, the dietitian will contribute important and unique services; services that can only be provided by a professional with detailed and thorough knowledge of nutrition—the dietitian. The dietitian must work extremely hard to acquire, maintain, and improve upon this knowledge. Opportunities will continue to expand, and the future in community dietetics is bright.

5

CONSULTANTS

CONSULTANTS WORK UNDER contract with health care facilities, in their own private practices, or for business and industry. They perform nutrition screening for their clients and offer advice on diet-related concerns such as weight loss or cholesterol reduction. Some work for wellness programs, sports teams, supermarkets, and other nutrition-related businesses. They may consult with food-service managers, providing expertise in sanitation, safety procedures, budgeting, and planning.

According to the ADA, the following are suggested roles the consulting dietitian performs:

Services provided to businesses or groups
- Evaluate and monitor food-service systems, making recommendations to provide nutritionally adequate food
- Develop budget proposals and recommend procedures for cost controls

- Plan, organize, and conduct orientation and in-service educational programs for food-service personnel
- Plan layout design and determine equipment requirements for food-service facilities
- Recommend and monitor standards for sanitation, safety, and security in food service
- Develop menu patterns
- Develop, maintain, and use pertinent record systems related to the needs of the organization and the consultant dietitian
- Provide guidance and evaluation of the job performance of dietetic personnel
- Maintain effective verbal and written communications and public relations, inter- and intradepartmentally

Services provided to individuals

- Assess, develop, implement, and evaluate nutritional care plans and provide for follow-up, including written reports
- Consult with and counsel clients regarding selection and procurement of food to meet optimal nutrition
- Develop menu patterns
- Develop, use, and evaluate educational materials related to services provided
- Consult with the health care team concerning the nutritional care of clients
- Interpret, evaluate, and utilize current research relating to nutritional care

Education

Education and experience necessary to practice as a consultant dietitian include:

1. Registration (R.D.)
2. One to four years of clinical or community nutrition experience
3. A master's degree in business and/or nutritional sciences (not required but it is suggested)

Private Practice

Dietitians in private practice work in the career areas discussed throughout this book. These areas provide population groups where consultant dietitians can market their services. As an example, a consultant might become involved in the employee health service of a corporation. For economic reasons, corporations are focusing on both preventive health care and education to decrease health care costs and increase worker productivity. By changing the employee's "health profile," a corporation can save money by cutting sick time, decreasing the use of medical care, and avoiding early retirement due to disablement.

Other areas for development of a private practice include:

- Physicians' offices or physicians' group
- Nursing homes/hospices
- Psychologists' groups
- Dental offices
- Weight-loss clinics
- Sports facilities
- Spas

Client Needs and Interests

To facilitate practice in these areas and others, the dietitian must determine: the nutrition needs and interests of clients, the format of counseling sessions, how to promote the service, how to build a client base, additional resources available for clients, who the competition is, and fees. Actual services provided may include:

- Weight reduction, weight maintenance, or weight gain nutrition counseling
- Nutrition education
- Obesity, diabetes, cardiovascular disease treatment
- Bulimia/anorexia counseling
- Premenstrual syndrome therapy
- Smoking cessation counseling and therapy
- Substance abuse nutrition therapy
- Publishing for newspapers and magazines
- Recipe analysis

Positive Aspects and Drawbacks

The positive aspects of a career in private practice include the ability to sell oneself and develop an assertive business profile; respect as a health professional from the medical community and the public; and the challenge to succeed on your own. Some drawbacks may be the financial risk and often having to rely on physician referral for patients. Also, payment for services may not be reimbursable by insurance companies. In addition, the general public may lack the knowledge to understand exactly what the dietitian can provide. Although there are obstacles, the highly self-motivated dietitian can develop a successful and rewarding independent practice.

Business and Industry

Business and industry may be considered the area with the most rapid growth for consultants. In the past, dietitians in business and industry typically worked for food companies developing new food products. Now, as "health" becomes a prominent focus in the private sector, opportunities for the dietitian seem limitless.

Industry recruiters, as well as executives in food-service management companies, report a continual need for dietitians in this area, especially those with management skills. Many businesses hire dietitians for their technical expertise, providing the company with a competitive edge in marketing its products and services. Also, public relations firms are hiring dietitians to help them provide nutrition information to their clients.

To take advantage of the available opportunities, dietitians need to expand their skills to include: management training, especially finance and marketing; oral, written, and media communication skills; and the ability to "sell" oneself to promote ideas and new projects and to improve the image of the profession.

A Marketable Profile

Recruiters and employers in this area are looking for the dietitian profile that projects:

- Self-confidence in professional knowledge and ability to learn new information
- An enthusiastic attitude about the job and about working
- An orientation toward achievement
- Assertive behavior in promotion of self, ideas, and products or services of employing corporation
- Willingness to travel or relocate
- Good communication skills
- Willingness to work long hours to accomplish a job
- Ability to utilize criticism for personal and professional growth

- Interest in upgrading and developing skills for advancement through a variety of continuing education programs

Education

The education required for an entry-level position in business and industry includes a B.S. from an approved dietetic program, registration, and management coursework. Management experience is valuable but not necessary in all cases. Also, coursework in accounting and personnel management is suggested. For the dietitian wanting to move into a middle or top management position, a master's degree in business administration (M.B.A.) is becoming necessary.

Specific skills and knowledge required when entering business and industry include finance, writing and communication skills, marketing, public speaking, computer efficiency, personnel management, budgeting and accounting, economics, food sciences, long-range planning and time management, and cost containment.

Types of Positions

Some of the positions available to the dietitian interested in practicing in business and industry include:

- Advertising, public relations, and marketing
- Anthropology research
- Architects or consultants to materials managers
- Chemical laboratory representatives
- Computer software development and sales
- Consumer affairs
- Cooking school instruction
- Equipment companies—service and sales
- Fitness and wellness centers, resorts, and spas
- Food brokers and distributors

- Hospital administration and management
- Lawyers involved with nutrition regulations, codes, and labor
- Nursing
- Personnel directors
- Pharmaceutical companies—sales, product development, marketing
- Product development—food and equipment
- Production manager
- Restaurant management
- Retail stores—food demonstration and cookware sales
- Social/nutrition programs—development, evaluation, and management

Sports and Cardiovascular Nutrition

Sports and cardiovascular dietitians usually begin with a clinical background as a registered dietitian and then obtain a master's degree of science in nutrition and exercise physiology. YMCAs, schools, universities, and businesses all provide a variety of opportunities to practice. The increased awareness of business and industry and of the general public about the importance of nutrition and exercise has contributed to this specialty's expansion.

Candidates are drawn to this area because of a personal interest in sports and because clients are actively seeking nutrition information. Work activities include individual diet/nutrition counseling, development of education materials and audiovisual aids, computer nutrient analysis, writing, and research.

As more is learned about the combined importance of nutrition and exercise, the demand for dietitians in this area will increase, and their work environments will expand to include hospitals, the community, and specialty work in professional and amateur athletics.

Food Product Companies

In food product companies, diverse career opportunities for dietitians are emerging in part due to the growing consumer desire for optimum health and child wellness. The dietitian provides a unique combination of practical aspects of diet and nutrition with the knowledge of food and the experience with consumers.

Typical food industry jobs for dietitians include research, product development, marketing, consumer science, recipe development, regulatory issues, labeling, and toxicology. In research, expectations involve extensive evaluation of dietary surveys, literature, patents, and other company products to determine needs and opportunities for new products. Interfacing with company lawyers may be part of the job, to provide a nutritional perspective on corporate communications, products developed, marketing strategies, or patents.

Skills necessary beyond technical expertise include the ability to discern the facts from many sources of information, to find gaps and opportunities, and to translate the science to the company audience. Communication and influencing skills are especially valuable, such as being able to succinctly present information with simple visual representation. Finally, flexibility is important, since timelines are often short and priorities can change.[1]

Sales

In this subspecialty, dietitians will sell a product and/or service. They may be employed by pharmaceutical, medical/nutritional, or food or food-service equipment or supplies companies. These companies utilize dietitians for their technical expertise regarding diet modification and food production and distribution. Dietitians have excellent opportunities as sales representatives because of their familiarity with the food and medicine industry. They have knowledge about medical therapy, know the language, and, therefore, can use a "soft-sell" approach. Additional skills required beyond technical expertise include skills in marketing, accounting, financial analysis, labor relations, and economics.

Fitness and Wellness

Fitness and wellness centers, resorts, and spas utilize dietitians for their menu planning and diet modification skills, as well as client nutrition education, disease awareness programs, weight-control classes, and writing for popular press, newsletters, and educational material development. Additional opportunities for the wellness dietitian include schools, recreational centers, and military bases.

The top ten skills needed by dietitians in wellness settings are communication, nutrition counseling, motivation/persuasion, needs assessment, facilitation of change in behavior, nutrition assessment, evaluation of individual success, use of technology, evaluation of program success, and promotional activities.[2] This area requires additional knowledge in marketing, finance, public relations, writing, and accounting as well as a well-rounded nutrition background that focuses on health maintenance, fitness, and physiologic measurement.

Communications

Dietitians are reaching a much wider audience through the field of nutrition communications. Every day, consumers and professionals access nutrition information through a variety of media: television and radio broadcasts, newspaper and magazine articles, public health campaigns, websites, books, newsletters, and brochures. This role to ensure that messages are communicated clearly, accurately, and effectively belongs to the registered dietitian, the acknowledged nutrition expert. The dietitian who possesses both nutrition knowledge and communications savvy is sought by public relations agencies, food companies, government agencies, magazine editors, and news directors.

Succeeding in the field of nutrition communications requires a special set of skills, including the following:

- Broad understanding of basic nutrition science and policy
- Ability to understand and interpret research data and provide context for laypeople
- Excellent written and verbal communication skills, including grammar, spelling, and sentence structure, as well as the ability to put scientific terms into "consumer speak"
- Ability to communicate to diverse groups of people

The nutrition communications dietitian may develop food and nutrition-related communications for consumer and/or professional audiences. These may include writing speeches and presentations; developing nutrition education materials, programs, and nutrition content for websites; developing or analyzing recipes; and public speaking to consumer and health professional audiences.[3]

As consumers and professionals alike continue to clamor for nutrition information, the future is indeed exciting for dietitians working as nutrition communicators. Registered dietitians trained in the field of communications are the best-qualified professionals to ensure that the nutrition messages of today—and tomorrow— are communicated accurately and effectively.[4]

6

ADDITIONAL OPPORTUNITIES IN NUTRITION

THE OPPORTUNITIES TO be found in nutrition cut a wide swath across many areas of expertise, including administration, public health, education, and the health professions.

The Administrative Dietitian

Many nutrition professionals are entering the field of food-service systems management. Here there is a need for the administrative dietitian, a management specialist. This area of dietetic practice includes many administrative and management responsibilities. Although this area may not sound dynamic, it has opportunities available for management growth, long-term job security and benefits, and the ability to develop experience that can be applied in other fields.

Management is the major function of the administrative dietitian, specifically, food-service systems management. This area of management is defined as the process of accomplishing food-service system objectives. These include menu planning and food procurement, production, distribution, and service.

Professional Roles

The roles performed by the entry-level dietitian in food-service systems management are delineated in the following list. These represent a combination of actual roles that currently exist and those that ought to exist. These roles are abstracted from a role delineation study for Foodservice Systems Management published by the American Dietetic Association.

The food-service systems management professional performs the following roles:

- Focuses food-service operations on nutrition goals of a target market
- Advances practitioner competence through self-improvement programs
- Promotes positive working relationships with others whose work has an impact on food-service systems
- Utilizes current food-service systems and nutrition information in management and research
- Manages food-service subsystems, including food procurement, production, distribution, and service
- Manages food-service system resources, including human, material, physical, and operational assets
- Manages quality assurance programs in area of responsibility
- Advocates action that advances food-service systems management and improves nutrition status of consumers

Education

The education required includes entry-level qualifications with three or fewer years of experience. Specific areas of study include:

- **Principles of food systems management.** Provides an overall view of the management of food systems, including personnel involved in food preparation and service; equipment for operation; the purchasing of food and supplies; and the management of time and money.
- **Quantity food purchasing and preparation.** Provides in-depth experience in menu planning, food preparation techniques, and cooking procedures to ensure quality food production.
- **Development, utilization, and maintenance of physical resources.** Provides education in planning a food-service facility, including how to write equipment specifications and prepare cost estimates, and equipment operation, sanitation, and preventive maintenance guidelines; with exposure to equipment salespeople, consultants, engineers, and architects in developing the layout plan.
- **Operations analysis.** Knowledge is gained in computer programming for use as a decision-making tool in food-service for cost containment, food purchasing, stock maintenance, and as a carry-over into clinical dietetics for modified diet menu planning and preparation.

Career Considerations

Job satisfaction is high when the administrative dietitian is able to assume several roles. These include a middle-management role as the director of a food-service system; an advisor role to top-level administrators of the organization; and a personnel administrator of other dietitians, food-service employees, and dietetic students.

Barriers to career development and expansion in this area include lack of visibility; the perception that dietitians, in general, lack adequate management skills; and the actual shortage of dietitians willing to assume management positions, which causes hospital and other administrators to look elsewhere to hire administrative personnel.

Public Health

Nutritional personnel working in public health are employed by health agencies at the federal, state, and local levels; they conduct needs assessments to establish priorities for nutrition programs affecting certain geographical populations or categories of people, such as children or pregnant women. Dietitians develop strategies for providing nutrition services; they implement the programs, evaluate and revise them, and establish new objectives.

Nutrition Services

Beginning in the mid-1960s, public health agencies increased direct nutrition services to populations at nutrition risk or with demonstrated nutrition needs, such as pregnant women, infants, and children. Services expanded so that by 1980, approximately one-half of the nutrition personnel in local health agencies were implementing WIC (Supplemental Food Program for Women, Infants, and Children), a direct service program. The federal WIC program is designed to establish a clear relationship between nutrition and health care services. The purpose of the program is to provide timely prenatal care to reduce the incidence of low-birth-weight infants.

At the federal level, there is a growing need for public health nutrition professionals to help prioritize nutrition issues and develop a clear focus in maternal nutrition. Therefore, there are opportunities for professionals to become involved in program development and implementation, along with nutrition research. Research is needed to establish baseline data on the nutrition and health status of the public, with special attention to infants, children, and the elderly. At the same time, plans must be developed for the assessment of remaining vulnerable groups such as adolescents, pregnant women, the handicapped, and the unemployed.

Also, community health centers, migrant health programs, and the expansion of primary health care have established additional work environments for the public health dietitian. These work environments include directing nutrition in state and local health departments with ambulatory clients in prevention and treatment centers.

Nutrition Education

The specialty of nutrition education provides many work environment opportunities. The three discussed here are nutrition education in the public school system, nutrition education in a fitness/health promotion program, and the cooperative extension specialist.

Nutrition Education in Schools

Nutrition education in the school system may involve working for the government at the state level to expand nutrition programs or with city school districts. To work in this area, four essential categories of expertise are important. These are:

Nutrition and Food

- Provide nutrition information to individuals and groups involved in education program development
- Use knowledge about school food service to conduct nutrition-related education programs

Education

- Work with teachers and food-service personnel to implement and evaluate nutrition programs
- Provide education programs and individual counseling to students

Communications

- Use various media (video, audio, radio) as an integral part of a nutrition education program
- Develop brochures, newsletters, or specific topic handouts to use as a part of a nutrition education program

Government

- Use the understanding about political processes as it relates to school food programs
- Write grants to fund nutrition education programs and counseling services

Health Promotion

The second area of nutrition education involves health promotion programs. Personal efforts to overcome smoking habits, alcohol and drug abuse, dietary excess, stress, and physical inactivity are evidence of the new health awareness in this country. As corporate America commits more resources to employee health promotion programs, due to their cost-effectiveness, more and more openings will become available for nutrition professionals to direct behavioral change programs.

The nutrition educator's roles in a fitness/health promotion program may include:

- Use of computer programs for nutrient analysis
- Interviews to obtain diet histories
- Interpretation of biochemical tests
- Percent body fat calculation and interpretation
- Evaluation of nutritional status
- Patient counseling to determine goals
- Development of tools for recording patient progress and maintaining documentation for research
- Group counseling and education
- Development of posters and pamphlets to use as education materials
- Workshops to deal with behavior change, cooking techniques, restaurant eating, holidays, and so forth
- Writing for lay publications

These roles may vary depending on the actual work environment; however, they are all important for any health promotion program.

Dietetic Curriculum Applicable to a Fitness Program[1]

Teaching
- Health risk analysis (health hazard appraisal) dealing with the risk of cardiovascular disease, diabetes, obesity, hypertension, and poor eating habits
- Nutrition as it relates to exercise physiology
- Nutrition and the athlete—current fads and practices

Skills

- Interviewing adapted to needs
- Interpretation of anthropometric measurements such as body (fat) composition as influenced by exercise
- Use and interpretation of computerized nutrient data
- Calculation of risk based on health risk analysis
- Generation of record system compatible with existing document systems
- Counseling/follow-up while in co-participant role
- Preparation/delivery of brief messages for impact in action-oriented setting
- Written communication through newsletters/audiovisuals
- Workshop planning and presentation based on group health needs and concerns
- Relationships with nontraditional health team (for example, exercise physiologists)
- Promotion of dietitian's role in fitness programs

The educational preparation necessary would include a B.S. or M.S. degree in nutrition with minor coursework in exercise physiology or another related field, such as psychology, counseling, business administration, or marketing.

Cooperative Extension Specialist

Cooperative Extension offices help the diverse populations of a state adapt to a rapidly changing society and improve their lives through an educational process that uses science-based knowledge. They focus on issues and needs relating to agriculture and the environment; management of natural resources; food safety and quality and health; family stability; economic security; and youth development.

The Cooperative Extension offices and programs are found within and affiliated with the state universities. For example, in the state of New Jersey, the Cooperative Extension programs are through Rutgers University at rce.rutgers.edu. There is a Cooperative Extension office located in each county. In New Jersey, there are twenty-one Cooperative Extension county offices.

Cooperative Extension specialists generate research-based information and solutions in the areas of agriculture, food and nutrition, environmental sciences and natural resources, and youth development. Their expertise and programs are delivered to the residents of each state. Their education and professional experience may be focused in food science, community nutrition, and research.

The work of the Cooperative Extension specialist includes:

- Developing, implementing, and evaluating educational programs and materials addressing family and community needs
- Conducting family and consumer educational programs
- Responding to general family, consumer, food safety, and food and nutrition questions

Additionally, Cooperative Extension specialists may provide valuable resource information to the dietitian, student, or career changer. They are extremely knowledgeable about the resources available in the community and can help provide educational materials, networking opportunities, as well as local job listings. Specialists also deal with many different socioeconomic groups and individuals with diverse cultural backgrounds.

Working with Other Health Professionals

A profession is defined as "a calling requiring specialized knowledge and often long and intensive academic preparation."[2] A professional "conforms to the technical or ethical standards of the profession . . . exhibiting a courteous, conscientious, and generally businesslike manner in the workplace."[3]

As a professional, the dietitian may interact with other professionals to provide the best care possible to the client. The team members may include a physician, pharmacist, physical therapist, nurse, psychologist, and others. The potential role of each will be discussed in relationship to the treatment of obesity. Other disease states such as heart disease, cancer, and autoimmune disease as well as medical conditions such as pregnancy may require similar treatment with the dietitian playing an important role as a health care team member.

Obesity

It is estimated that two-thirds of Americans are overweight or obese, and four hundred thousand preventable deaths are annually attributed to obesity.[4] Obesity therapy requires psychological, medical, physical fitness, and dietary management. The concept of the team approach is imperative for the successful treatment of this problem. Also, there are multiple treatment choices for the individual dealing with this health problem. It is important that the client be educated about the choices available. The dietitian may play a critical role in this process. The dietitian may be responsible for the patient's total care and may act as the coordinator of all team efforts.

In this approach, the dietitian may be responsible for medical monitoring, behavioral and cognitive counseling, and nutrition education. The medical role of the dietitian may be to take blood pressure, weigh the patient weekly, develop an eating/diet plan, and order appropriate lab tests, or the dietitian may delegate these roles to the dietetic technician who is registered. As she or he monitors these aspects, problems can be related back to the dietitian and physician to ensure complete medical care. Depending on the presence of physical injury, a physical therapist may be consulted.

It is important for the dietitian to develop a relationship with the patient so that personal problems can be discussed. Basic counseling techniques may be used to help patients better understand their behavior. The dietitian may also be qualified to identify more serious psychological problems and refer the patient to a psychologist or psychiatrist.

Other ways in which the dietitian may interact with allied health professionals include:

- Consultation with a pharmacist to discuss drug-nutrient interaction, vitamin/mineral supplementation, or parenteral and enteral product use
- Interaction with a nurse to attain information regarding actual patient progress and home health care problems
- Participation with other specialty dietitians to provide education for preventive care for other diseases and conditions

To help the patient transition from the hospital to home, the dietitian may interact with:

- A social worker to help establish home services
- A "Meals on Wheels" provider to ensure food availability
- A dietitian in private practice to transition nutrition services to the home

- An exercise physiologist to initiate an exercise program at home or make a referral to a local fitness facility

The dietitian requires medical and psychological training as well as traditional clinical dietetic experience. The dietitian must also be knowledgeable about the total care services provided at the hospital or medical facility. As well, he or she must be informed about the services available in the local community.

Conclusion

Current and future technology will aid in the development of new administrative roles and challenges. The administrative dietitian must be willing to sacrifice traditional approaches and adopt new methods to deal with cost containment, while maintaining quality food service, increased productivity, and an increase in food and clinical nutrition services. To meet these challenges, the administrative dietitian must be assertive, knowledgeable, willing to work long and hard hours, and be goals-oriented.

The areas of public health nutrition and nutrition education are providing constant stimulation due to the diversity of work environments and work situations. For the dietitian not interested in the "traditional" clinical nutrition approach, these areas will continue to grow and challenge him or her to implement new ideas and programs.

As a professional working with other health team members, the dietitian must be confident, knowledgeable, and able to apply all acquired skills to provide treatment to patients. The dietitian must also effectively communicate with other professionals as well as specialty dietitians within the field.

7

THE DIETETIC TECHNICIAN

IT IS GENERALLY recognized that dietitians need assistance in performing their professional responsibilities. Dietetic technicians are technically skilled individuals who have been prepared to assume a supportive nutrition role and work under the guidance of a registered dietitian.

The registered dietitian oversees the assessment, planning, and evaluation of individual patients, with a dietetic technician assisting in any or all phases of the nutrition care process. The dietetic technician has responsibilities in assigned areas of nutrition care, such as dietary instruction of selected individuals, consultation with the health team, and monitoring of patient food quality and acceptance.

Responsibilities

The American Dietetic Association recognizes these roles as appropriate for the dietetic technician who has completed an approved associate degree program (see Appendix D).

At the *client* level, the clinical dietetic technician assists the registered dietitian in clinical practice to provide direct nutrition services to patients. The technician is responsible for:

- Using predetermined criteria in screening patients to identify those at nutritional risk and collecting data for use in assessing dietary status
- Following guidelines established by the registered dietitian to develop nutrition care plans for individual patients
- Providing technical services in the implementation of nutrition care plans
- Monitoring the effect of nutrition intervention and assessing patient food acceptance
- Providing diet counseling and education to individuals not at nutritional risk

At the second, or *intraprofessional*, level, the dietetic technician cooperates with the clinical dietitian in promoting standards of practice and using current knowledge to solve nutrition problems of individual patients.

At the third, or *interprofessional*, level, the technician is responsible for coordinating the nutrition care of assigned patients with other health services and coordinating designated nutrition care plans with institutional food-service activities.

At the *intraorganizational* level, the dietetic technician utilizes established standards and procedures to implement the system of patient nutrition care. This responsibility includes:

- Utilizing established procedures for making available designated special food products and dietary supplements
- Supervising diet clerks and other patient food-service personnel
- Developing and implementing a program of orientation, training, and in-service education for patient food-service personnel

Employment

Employment environments for the dietetic technician include community hospitals, intermediate or skilled nursing facilities, and university medical centers. This indicates that health care is the primary employment outlet. For example, a dietetic technician may work as a junior research coordinator creating client questionnaires, managing questionnaires, writing abstracts, and collecting data to be analyzed by the registered dietitian. A dietetic technician may have more time to spend with each individual patient, allowing the dietitian to focus on more acute-care patients. The dietetic technician may focus on keeping people healthy through appropriate food choices and stressing the importance of good nutritional status.

Like the registered dietitian specializing in specific areas, the dietetic technician is expanding into subspecialties. These subspecialties may include work in:

- Clinical psychiatric areas
- Pediatric practice
- Critical care
- Food-service management
- Community programs
- Wellness centers
- Business and industry

Education

The dietetic technician is a professional who holds an associate of arts degree and has completed 450 hours of supervised experience in the area of either nutrition care or food-service management. The technician is viewed as the assistant to the clinical dietitian or the public health nutritionist. The approved program of dietetic technician education prepares the technician to conduct patient interviews; to assist patients in the daily choice of a balanced diet; to give routine dietary instructions; to arrange meal plans for modified diets; to assist patients in health care institutions or clients in the community in meal planning and food purchasing for the entire family; and to assist the dietitian or nutritionist in preparing educational materials for various teaching programs.

The following sample represents the recommended American Dietetic Association pattern for an approved program of dietetic technician education leading to competency in nutrition care.

Sample Dietetic Technician Nutrition Care Program

Course	Semester Hours
Semester One	
Nutrition Care I	3
Supervised Field Experience	1
Foods	3
Health Field	1
Contemporary Sociology	3
Open Course	3
Open Course	3
Total	17

Semester Two

Nutrition Care II	3
Supervised Field Experience	2
Education	3
Health Field	1
Open Course	3
Open Course	3
Total	15

Semester Three

Nutrition Care III	3
Supervised Field Experience	3
Health Care Delivery Systems	3
Management	3
Open Course	3
Total	15

Semester Four

Nutrition Care IV	3
Supervised Field Experience	4
Dietetic Seminar	1
Open Course	3
Open Course	3
Open Course	3
Total	17

In Nutrition Care I, students study normal nutrition. This course covers why and how people eat; what influences malnutrition; how to bring about changes in food habits; cultural food patterns; the nature of food and its work in the body; the normal process of digestion, absorption, and metabolism; nutrients and their functions; nutrition in the life cycle; and food fads.

Nutrition Care II covers the study of diet therapy. This course is concerned with the nutritional care of the patient who has problems of the upper gastrointestinal region and progresses to nutritional care of patients with congestive heart failure, hypertension, atherosclerosis, hyperlipidemia, obesity, and diabetes.

Nutrition Care III involves study of the general problems of nutritional care of patients with problems of digestion, absorption, and metabolism, and fluid and electrolyte balance.

Nutrition Care IV emphasizes community nutrition learning to deal with inborn errors of metabolism, anemia, arthritis, and more.

The Foods course considers an overview of foods; the basic food groups; principles of menu planning and food purchasing for the home, including budgeting; food stamps; and interpretation of food advertising and labels. It also covers food additives, food sanitation and spoilage, unit pricing, and FDA rulings.

Dietetic Seminar introduces the health field and the roles of practitioners in dietetics. The student is also introduced to various feeding systems and the team efforts to provide adequate nutrition care.

The Future

The future of employment as a dietetic technician is expanding as the increased utilization of the technician by various organizations will lead to cost containment, better use of supportive personnel, reduction in staffing needs, and functioning of dietitians at the level of proficiency for which they were educated.

8

SALARIES AND JOB
SATISFACTION

THIS CHAPTER WILL give you an idea of the earnings and benefits you can expect working in nutrition.

Salaries

The American Dietetic Association published the 2002 Dietetics Compensation and Benefits Survey[1] in response to member requests for "objective, reliable information about industry norms for pay and benefit levels for the dietetic professions." The tables presented in the 2002 Dietetics Compensation and Benefits Survey provide salary information based on survey results for registered dietitians and dietetic technicians, registered. These tables illustrate the relative effects of various components in determining a dietetics professional's salary. The components are as follows:

- Years in field
- Years in position
- Education level and years in field
- Credentials held
- ADA membership
- Practice area and years in field
- Employment setting
- Employer status
- Size of organization
- Responsibility level and number supervised
- Location

The factors showing the strongest association with compensation levels for registered dietitians include number of years of experience, level of supervisory responsibility, budget responsibility, and practice area. Clinical and community positions tend to pay less, whereas consultation and business positions pay more.

Compensation for Registered Dietitians

Among all registered dietitians in all positions, the median hourly wage as of April 1, 2002, was $22 per hour. This equates to a salary of $47,760 per year. The 2002 Dietetics Compensation and Benefits Survey reported median salary ranges for selected specialty and advanced practice dietitians as:

| | Salary | | |
Practice Area	Bachelor's degree	Master's degree	Specialty
Registered dietitian	$40,000	$40,900	$45,000
Pediatrics	$39,000	$43,100	$46,800
Renal	$44,000	$45,000	$46,000
Diabetes educator	$42,200	$41,700	$47,300
Nutrition support	$42,600	$48,300	$45,700

Education

Education beyond the bachelor's degree is clearly associated with wage gains. Overall, the difference between the median wage of registered dietitians with a bachelor's degree and that of registered dietitians with a master's degree is $2.30 per hour; positions for which the differential associated with a master's degree exceeds that value include clinical dietitian, long-term care; research dietitian; school/child care nutritionist; executive-level professional; director of food and nutrition services; assistant food-service director; and director of nutrition.

Nonacademic Positions

The highest-paying nonacademic positions held primarily by registered dietitians include:

	Median hourly wage	Median yearly salary
Executive-level professional	$34.86	$77,000
Research and development nutritionist	$30.30	$64,400
Public relations or marketing professional	$29.43	$62,500
Director of nutrition	$29.23	$67,500
School/child care nutritionist	$26.44	$52,900
Sales representative	$25.96	$70,000
Consultant—communications	$25.73	$52,500
Director of food and nutrition services	$25.07	$53,000
Clinical nutrition manager	$25.00	$51,900
Consultant—community/corporate	$25.00	$47,100

Compensation for Dietetic Technicians, Registered

In 2002, the estimated median annual incomes for dietetic technicians for the three most common areas of practice were: clinical nutrition, $30,000; food and nutrition management, $34,000; and long-term care, $29,000. (Salary levels may vary with geographical location, scope of responsibility, credentials held, education, and years in position.) Among all dietetic technicians, registered, in all positions, the median hourly wage as of April 1, 2002, was $14.74 per hour; if annualized, this equals a salary of $30,660 per year. The highest-paying positions held by substantial numbers of dietetic technicians, registered, include:

	Median hourly wage	Median yearly salary
Director of food and nutrition services	$18.03	$40,000
Clinical dietitian, long-term care	$15.39	$32,000
Dietetic technician, food service	$15.38	$32,900

Factors showing the strongest association with compensation levels for dietetic technicians, registered, include number of years of experience, budget responsibility, size of organization, and practice area. The dietetic technicians, registered, who go beyond the required associate's degree to earn a bachelor's degree receive nearly an extra dollar per hour in median wage.

Negotiation Skills

Salary and compensation negotiations are the most important negotiations in your life. They affect professional and personal well-being, and the objective should be to maximize your own gain. Convince the employer that you are the best candidate; show the employer you are the one he or she really wants, and do so in a way that is respectful and constructive.

The majority of employers expect candidates to negotiate, so 90 percent of employers do not include all of the value they are willing to offer for a position in the first offer. If you accept the first offer as made, you are not claiming the value that you could have obtained. The vast majority of employers prefer the negotiators who believe they can do the job better than most people because of their personal skills, education, and experience. When you negotiate effectively, you are modeling exactly the kinds of skills, personality traits, and strategies that employers want.

Negotiation is a productive decision-making process. It is not one that necessarily instils conflict. A lot of the art of negotiation has to do with how you approach it personally. You can be very warm and direct and respectful of the employer, but it doesn't mean you have to make unnecessary concessions and compromises. You can assert yourself, ask for what you want, and still be extremely likable and personable.

If you want something, and the employer is not offering it up front, you'd better ask for it. In addition, you need to realize that what you get paid is a combination of what you are worth and whether you negotiate, and if you do negotiate, how successfully you do so. Therefore, if you want to have the salary compensation that you believe you are entitled to, you have to learn to negotiate effectively.[2]

Additional Benefits

Other areas of compensation that should be included when considering positions are employee benefits. These benefits are a valuable asset to the nutrition professional. Additional benefits may include:

- Disability benefits and sick and mental health leave; insurance group life, accident, hospitalization; other
- Twelve days' sick leave per year

- Group life insurance equal to annual salary; hospitalization and medical insurance
- Dental insurance
- Discounts on goods and services purchased from company
- Employee meals
- Profit sharing
- Special bonuses
- Vacation and holidays
- Plan for salary increments and opportunities for advancement
- Retirement plans
- Professional growth; for example, attendance at professional meetings, education, sabbaticals
- Travel allowances
- Employee fitness program and facility

As a prospective nutrition professional, it is important to check with area practice groups about current salaries and benefits. Another resource is the classified ad section of the *Journal of the American Dietetic Association*. This section will provide regional salaries for current openings in the field and the qualifications necessary.

Job Satisfaction

In today's ever-expanding and changing job market, it is becoming more important to choose a career that will provide stimulation and rewards. Nutrition is definitely one of these career choices.

There are multiple aspects of a job that lead to job satisfaction. These considerations include interest in the work, goals that are reasonable, work that is mentally challenging and not too physically demanding, tasks that can be successfully completed, acknowledgment of work well done, a cooperative environment, and work that builds self-esteem.

Finally, it is important for the nutrition professional to evaluate all aspects of the potential job to determine if the employer can provide the satisfying work environment and work experience for the development of a rewarding career. The time has come when it is the professionals' responsibility to determine whether they are right for the job and whether they can enthusiastically tackle the job expectations to achieve job satisfaction.

9

PRACTITIONER PROFILES

NUTRITION CONTINUES TO be a rapidly growing discipline ranging in content from agriculture and animal sciences to human medicine. Because of our own particular interests, training, and experience, each person in the field tends to see only a small portion of the full spectrum of nutrition. In an attempt to provide the interested student with as broad a spectrum as possible, we have profiled dietitians who are currently practicing. We learn about their work environments and work roles, the education pathway they followed, previous work experience, and the future.

Gail A. Levey, M.S., R.D., Communications Consultant

Gail currently specializes in nutrition communication. She has reported the nutrition news weekly on WCBS-TV's "Channel 2 News at Noon" and was formerly on-air nutrition contributor to "CBS Morning News." She was the nutritionist for the "Weight

Watchers Magazine" television show, now on videotape. Gail has discussed nutrition on the "Joan Rivers Show," the "Today Show," "Good Morning America," "WABC-TV News," the Cable News Network, and Lifetime Television. She has appeared on television and radio stations across the country.

Gail is also a writer who contributes articles to major magazines, including *Parade*, *American Health*, *Good Food*, *Health*, *Seventeen*, *Weight Watchers Magazine*, and *Vegetarian Times*. She has researched articles for other writers, written nutrition booklets, lectured, and consulted for businesses.

Her undergraduate education was in nutritional sciences at Cornell University, and she completed her M.S. in nutrition and public health at Columbia University. She completed a six-month work experience to qualify to take the registration exam. Gail suggests that dietitians develop in the following ways if they expect to have a varied practice:

- Obtain a nutrition/biochemistry education base
- Acquire an advanced degree in a related area
- Associate with good mentors and peers
- Keep up-to-date with current trends and food product development
- Strive to be visible in the media and outspoken at work
- Develop writing skills

To achieve career goals, Gail states, "Versatility is the key to staying power. Be a dietitian but hone writing skills. Know sports nutrition and exercise physiology, too. Practice cardiovascular nutrition but know the mechanics of a stress test and how to take blood pressure. The more diverse your skills, the more valuable you become."

Maureen Serrano, R.D., Business and Industry Consultant

Maureen provides various nutrition services to a number of different organizations. She is the administrative director for a disease-prevention and health-promotion program, she consults for specialty clinics at a university-based hospital, she is a lecturer for a major airline, and she provides services to children and adults who have developmental disabilities and to a large physician practice group that includes adult medicine, pediatrics, and obstetrics and gynecology.

Maureen's work roles are diverse. She develops and implements programs on health promotion and disease prevention, which include body composition testing, fitness testing, computerized dietary analysis, and lifestyle assessment. She also develops menus and therapeutic diets for persons with special needs, counsels patients, and lectures on healthy eating.

Maureen obtained her B.S. degree in human nutrition and dietetics and completed a dietetic internship to obtain her R.D. status. This gave her a broad focus on nutrition, since her internship was a combination of administrative, clinical, and food-service roles.

Maureen finds that her consulting business allows her the flexibility to combine her varied work experiences and interests with her goal as a wife and mother. She believes that organization is crucial to a successful business and gives the client a sense of one's expertise. Displaying a positive self-image also transmits a dedication to health, and effective communication skills transmit a clear message. In addition, networking with dietitians and other health professionals helps to establish a strong professional foundation, which is essential for the dietitian who chooses to pursue a career as a consultant.

Cathy Powers, M.S., R.D., Curriculum Development, The Culinary Institute of America

Cathy received her B.S. degree in dietetics from Indiana University of Pennsylvania and her M.S. degree in restaurant and hotel management at Purdue University, Indiana. She was then employed by The Culinary Institute of America in Hyde Park, New York. Her challenge was to develop a nutrition program throughout the culinary curriculum. The outcome was a restaurant concept that incorporated the nutrition principles—low fat, salt, and cholesterol; moderate protein; and high carbohydrate—with classical culinary techniques and standards. The concept eventually included computer nutrient analysis of guest menus and recipes, and a state grant provided funding for computers for student use.

Now Cathy teaches Culinary Institute students, corporate chefs, major hotel-chain food-service personnel, the military, school systems, and others how to implement nutrition concepts in the kitchen. Additionally, The Culinary Institute has published a nutritional cooking book and a series of videotapes.

Cathy believes that the future is food—specifically, teaching individuals how to implement nutrition principles in the kitchen. The objectives are to teach chefs how to offer healthy alternatives, make them aware of portion sizes, and educate service staff about healthy menu options.

Cathy's advice for the dietetic student is, "Don't be afraid to create your own path. There are opportunities waiting for the person willing to open the door and take a route not tried before." Cathy believes that essential skills include computer knowledge, writing, public speaking, foods knowledge and preparation, and "people management." In addition, Cathy believes it is important to be aware of new food products and labeling standards.

Janet Helm, M.S., R.D., Nutritionist, McDonald's Corporation

Janet is currently the nutritionist for McDonald's Corporation. Her major role is to strengthen the nutrition function of product development to maintain nutrient analysis of products and to determine how to communicate nutrition information to the customer.

Janet received her B.S. degree in home economics and mass communications and her M.S. degree from Kansas State University. She then pursued a six-month work experience to qualify to take the R.D. exam, spending half of the time at a hospital and the other half at an NBC-affiliate television station. She entered the profession as a dietetic technician at a hospital where she obtained valuable experience as a nutrition educator. She wrote for the hospital newsletter and developed patient education materials and community nutrition classes.

After her six-month work experience, Janet went on to work for the Greater Kansas City Dairy Council (affiliated with the National Dairy Council). She then became an account executive/nutrition specialist for Ketchum Public Relations in New York City. While at Ketchum, Janet worked on several food-related accounts including the National Livestock and Meat Board, the California Prune Board, American Egg Board, Hoffman LaRoche's Vitamin Nutrition Information Service, and in Ketchum's test kitchen, developing and analyzing recipes. Additionally, Janet was involved with developing press materials and consumer brochures, and she organized nutrition conferences for Ketchum clients.

For the future, Janet states, "Nutrition is only going to continue to be an important issue. We must work hard to maintain traditional roles while we also build in other areas." Janet believes that nutrition opportunities are growing in the areas where the nutrition professional uses his or her skills and background in different settings, such as public relations, restaurant management, food product development, and marketing.

Amy Barr, M.S., R.D., Director of Nutrition, Diet, and Fitness, Good Housekeeping Institute

Amy is involved with clearing all advertising that has anything to do with nutrition, including food labeling, calorie content, and nutrition claims, and with checking recipes. She also writes a column called "What's News: Nutrition, Diet, and Fitness" for the institute. In addition, she is involved in radio and TV tours that discuss current nutrition issues. The institute also provides the computer-based software information on all the recipes published in the magazine. The institute currently employs one other dietitian, a home economist, and a kitchen technician.

Amy received her B.S. in home economics with a major in nutrition at the University of Nebraska, and completed a master's degree in nutrition at Tufts University and master's in science journalism at Boston University.

Amy says that the hospital setting is not for everyone. Future job expansion includes nutrition positions in advertising, marketing, public relations, and other areas of business. She feels that additional coursework in business management, advertising, and communications is important for the future nutrition professional.

Virginia Aronson, M.S., R.D., Nutritionist/Writer

Virginia works as the nutritionist/writer for the Harvard Department of Nutrition. She writes nutrition education materials for lay individuals and professionals. She has also written nine books and writes a monthly column for *Runners World* and *Shape* magazines.

Her education began at the University of Vermont, where she received her B.S. in dietetics (a traditional program). She completed her internship in New York and received her M.S. in nutrition, with an emphasis in education, from Framingham State University. Following completion of her M.S. degree, she worked for the Community Health Education Department, developing and implementing weight-control clinics, group workshops, and lectures.

Virginia believes that additional coursework in education, writing, and communication, and practice in working with the media would be helpful to achieve a rewarding career. She perceives that a nutrition career will expand into public education–related areas, such as fitness centers, preventive/wellness education, and nutrition writing and related communications.

Rita Warren, M.S., R.D., Manager, Nutrition Technical Services, General Mills

Rita acts as the consultant for nutrition resources for internal groups within General Mills, Inc. Her department looks at the nutrition impact of products and nutrition labeling, and the department also discusses nutrition concerns with marketing. Other areas include providing nutrition education to health professionals via a newsletter, pamphlets, and booklets, and providing nutrition education to schools. There are ten nutritionists employed by the department. All have at least an M.S. degree and are registered dietitians or R.D.-qualified.

Rita received her undergraduate degree in food science with a minor in chemistry, and her M.S. degree in nutrition with a minor in food science. She worked in the food chemistry lab at the University of Minnesota, then went to Pillsbury and worked on chemical analysis of foods.

Rita believes the skills that are important for future career development include knowledge about computers, communications, business, and government nutrition policies.

Carole Shore, M.S., R.D., Technical Information Specialist, National Agricultural Library

Carole has a unique position as a librarian. There are only a few library staffs that she is aware of who have selected nutrition professionals and trained them in library management so they can provide nutrition-related services. Some of these are:

- The National Agricultural Library
- The Congressional Research Service
- The National Medical Library

There are two major work areas—acquisitions and reference. Acquisitions is the process of selecting the books, journals, and audiovisuals that the library will obtain and catalog. Reference librarians are subject matter specialists who help clients obtain the information they are interested in. They will also index, abstract material, and work with computers to provide short bibliographical data on nutrition topics. Carole currently works with three other registered dietitians.

Carole's educational background includes a B.S. in dietetics following a traditional program with an internship. Her M.S. degree was completed in medical dietetics at Ohio State University. Her previous work experience included research with the United States Department of Agriculture, developing United States Dietary Goals.

Carole believes the future nutrition student should choose a career that provides the potential to "ladder" or move upward in responsibility and authority. There is a need to combine two disciplines, for example, dietetics and information science or dietetics and management. She perceives growth potential in public health and community nutrition because of the increase in hospital costs and the aging population. Also, Carole believes that the information explosion will create a greater need in library sciences.

Linda Houtkooper, Ph.D., R.D., Nutrition Research Specialist

As a lecturer, Linda has taught undergraduate studies in nutrition as it applies to life. This work involved organizing visual aids, writing lectures, evaluating student projects and progress, and providing student counseling. As a writer, Linda currently writes for *Swimming World* magazine, where she contributes a monthly column on questions related to nutrition and swimming performance. She also writes feature nutrition articles for *Swim Magazine* and has developed videotapes titled *Winning Sports Nutrition 1: The Train-*

ing Diet and *2: The Competition Diet.* In addition to writing for lay publications, Linda has written for professional journals. A recent publication discussed body composition assessment methods for children, using bioelectrical impedance.

As a consultant, Linda has provided nutrition advice for program development at the Gatorade Sports Sciences Institute; has provided sports nutrition information to aerobic instructors' workshops; has developed and implemented a nutrition weight management course for an employee fitness program; and has done literature review/research to update paraprofessionals.

Linda received her B.S. in home economic education with a minor in guidance and counseling. Her Ph.D. is in nutritional sciences with a minor in exercise physiology. Her research involves validation of new methods of analysis for body composition, assessment of the nutritional status of elite female athletes, and determining the effects of resistance weight training on bone mineral content of healthy young women.

When asked about the future, Linda says that she sees nutrition evolving in interdisciplinary areas. She foresees dietitians working with behavior therapists, exercise physiologists, pharmacists, and physicians; and doing research and program development for the community, in business and industry, and at universities.

Conclusion

It is exciting to learn about the variety of positions available for the nutrition professional. It is evident that career opportunities can provide a rewarding work environment and the ability to develop as a team member. A formalized education program, registration status, continuing education, and a mentor/peer group are all essential for the development of the nutrition professional.

10

DIETETIC EDUCATION

THERE ARE SEVERAL education and experience routes that can be taken toward becoming a dietitian. The major education routes accredited or approved by the American Dietetic Association are didactic programs, postbaccalaureate dietetic internships, coordinated undergraduate programs, and pre-professional practice programs (AP4).

The American Dietetic Association Commission on Accreditation accredits the coordinated undergraduate programs and dietetic internships in a process requiring site surveys. The American Dietetic Association staff approves the other two programs after a paper review; there is no formal accreditation of those programs.

Each of these approved education programs will be discussed in detail in this chapter.[1]

Didactic Programs

These programs consist of a formalized baccalaureate degree offered at an accredited college or university and are approved by the American Dietetic Association.

The didactic programs represent the current academic standards for the educational preparation of the professional dietitian. The actual academic requirements for completion of the program can be requested from the colleges and universities listed in Appendix B.

Graduates of didactic programs who are verified by the program director may apply for dietetic internships or pre-professional practice programs to establish eligibility for active membership in the American Dietetic Association and/or to complete the registration examination.

Knowledge and Skills for Didactic Programs

Individuals interested in becoming registered dietitians should expect to study a wide variety of topics focusing on food, nutrition, and management. These areas are supported by the sciences: physical and biological, behavioral and social, and communication. Becoming a dietitian involves a combination of academic preparation, including a minimum of a baccalaureate degree, and a supervised practice component.

The following foundation knowledge and skill requirements are listed in the eight areas that students will focus on in the academic component of a dietetics program. Foundation learning is divided as follows: basic knowledge of a topic, working or in-depth knowledge of a topic as it applies to the profession of dietetics, and ability to demonstrate the skill at a level that can be developed further.

To successfully achieve the foundation knowledge and skills, graduates must demonstrate the ability to communicate and collaborate, solve problems, and apply critical thinking skills.

These requirements may be met through separate courses, combined into one course, or as part of several courses as determined by the college or university sponsoring a program accredited or approved by the Commission on Accreditation/Approval for Dietetics Education (CAADE) of the American Dietetic Association.

Communications

Graduates will have basic knowledge about:

- Negotiation techniques
- Lay and technical writing
- Media presentations

Graduates will have working knowledge of:

- Interpersonal communication skills
- Counseling theory and methods
- Interviewing techniques
- Educational theory and techniques
- Concepts of human and group dynamics
- Public speaking
- Educational materials development

Graduates will have demonstrated the ability to:

- Present an educational session for a group
- Counsel individuals on nutrition

- Demonstrate a variety of documentation methods
- Explain a public policy position regarding dietetics
- Use current information technologies
- Work effectively as a team member

Physical and Biological Sciences

Graduates will have basic knowledge about:

- Exercise physiology
- Organic chemistry
- Biochemistry
- Physiology
- Microbiology
- Nutrient metabolism
- Pathophysiology related to nutrition care
- Fluid and electrolyte requirements
- Pharmacology: nutrient-nutrient and drug-nutrient interaction

Graduates will have demonstrated the ability to:

- Interpret medical terminology
- Interpret laboratory parameters relating to nutrition
- Apply microbiological and chemical considerations to process controls

Social Sciences

Graduates will have basic knowledge about:

- Public policy development
- Psychology

- Health behaviors and educational needs
- Economics and nutrition

Research

Graduates will have basic knowledge about:

- Research methodologies
- Needs assessments
- Outcomes-based research
- Scientific method
- Quality improvement methods

Graduates will have demonstrated the ability to:

- Interpret current research
- Interpret basic statistics

Food

Graduates will have basic knowledge about:

- Food technology
- Biotechnology
- Culinary techniques
- Sociocultural and ethnic food consumption issues and trends for various consumers
- Food safety and sanitation
- Food delivery systems
- Food and nonfood procurement
- Availability of nutrition programs in the community
- Formulation of local, state, and national food security policy
- Food production systems

- Environmental issues related to food
- Role of food in promotion of a healthy lifestyle
- Promotion of pleasurable eating
- Food and nutrition laws/regulations/policies
- Food availability and access for the individual, family, and community
- Applied sensory evaluation of food

Graduates will have demonstrated the ability to:

- Calculate and interpret nutrient composition of foods
- Translate nutrition needs into menus for individuals and groups
- Determine recipe/formula proportions and modifications for volume food production
- Write specifications for food and food-service equipment
- Apply food science knowledge to functions of ingredients in food
- Demonstrate basic food preparation and presentation skills
- Modify recipe/formula for individual or group dietary needs

Nutrition

Graduates will have basic knowledge about:

- Alternative nutrition and herbal therapies
- Evolving methods of assessing health status
- Influence of age, growth, and normal development on nutritional requirements
- Nutrition and metabolism
- Assessment and treatment of nutritional health risks

- Medical nutrition therapy, including alternative feeding modalities, chronic diseases, dental health, mental health
- Strategies to assess need for adaptive feeding techniques and equipment
- Health promotion and disease prevention theories and guidelines
- Influence of socioeconomic, cultural, and psychological factors on food and nutrition behavior

Graduates will have demonstrated the ability to:

- Calculate and/or define diets for common conditions, i.e., health conditions addressed by health promotion/disease prevention activities or chronic diseases of the general population, such as hypertension, obesity, diabetes, and diverticular disease
- Screen individuals for nutritional risk
- Collect pertinent information for comprehensive nutrition assessments
- Determine nutrient requirements across the lifespan, i.e., infants through geriatrics and a diversity of people, culture, and religions
- Measure, calculate, and interpret body composition data
- Calculate parenteral and enteral nutrition formulations

Management

Graduates will have basic knowledge about:

- Program planning, monitoring, and evaluation
- Strategic management

- Facility management
- Organizational change theory
- Risk management
- Management theories
- Human resource management, including labor relations
- Materials management
- Financial management, including accounting principles
- Quality improvement
- Information management
- Systems theory
- Marketing theory and techniques
- Diversity issues

Graduates will have demonstrated the ability to:

- Determine costs of services/operation
- Prepare a budget
- Interpret financial data
- Apply marketing principles

Health Care Systems

Graduates will have basic knowledge about:

- Health care policy and administration
- Health care delivery systems
- Current reimbursement issues
- Ethics of care

Dietetic Internships

The dietetic internship is a formalized postbaccalaureate educational program. It is sponsored and conducted by various organizations outside of educational institutions and is accredited by the ADA. Curriculums are designed to provide classroom and supervised clinical experiences to meet qualifications for dietetic practice. Students are required to enroll in an accredited internship following completion of the didactic program to qualify for taking the written registration examination.

Entrance into dietetic internships is not guaranteed. The number of applicants is presently greater than the available positions. Therefore, it is important to be aware of the applicant selection processes. The criteria for student selection used by most institutions include academic record, which is the most heavily weighted; letters of recommendation; student essays; and work experience.

Academic Records

The grade point average (GPA) carries a relatively heavy weight. Educators view past academic success as a valid and reliable predictor of continued academic success. Success in an internship program depends upon a firm academic base. Among the relevant subject areas, grade point averages in science and English are considered good indicators of likelihood of success because of the strong emphasis on science and on written and oral communication skills in dietetics.

Letters of Recommendation

Letters of recommendation provide a means of learning about an individual's abilities in many areas. Most institutions usually request three letters, including character references from a professor in a major discipline, an academic advisor, a department chairperson, an instructor in a science course, or employers in professionally related jobs.

Student Essays

Student essays are used to gather information about an applicant's motivation, goals, and depth of interest in the profession. Typical essays include professional goals, reasons for choosing dietetics as a profession, reasons for choosing the institution's internship program, and personal strengths and weaknesses.

Work Experience

Work experience ensures that the applicants have an understanding of the actual work performed and that they have a continuing interest in the profession. Volunteer work is as important as paid employment at this stage of the career.

Other Variables

Other selection variables include:

- **Conceptual ability.** Quality of written and oral expression, ability to master new information and skills, ability to understand complex new theories, and ability to translate theory into practice are important considerations.

- **Overall preparation.** Relevance and quality of the applicant's previous educational experiences in school, in work, and in extracurricular activities; courses and electives taken as an undergraduate; any refresher and/or advanced study are also considered.
- **Self-direction.** Essential skills include the ability to set goals, organize one's own activities, and work independently.
- **Leadership ability.** Formal recognition of leadership through election to office and honors and informal recognition by peers and others at school, work, and in extracurricular and community activities are indications of potential for success.
- **Ability to perform under pressure.** Flexibility, the ability to set priorities, the ability to set goals and organize work, physical stamina, and the ability to remain reasonably calm under stress are evaluated. The overall load carried by a student during college (academic, work, and extracurricular family or community responsibilities) is considered.
- **Interpersonal skills.** Realistic self-confidence, the ability to sense the mood and concerns of others, appropriate use and interpretation of both verbal and nonverbal communications, the ability to adapt to a variety of people and situations, and concern for the well-being of others are also important.

Coordinated Undergraduate Programs

The coordinated undergraduate program consists of four years of undergraduate study, with coordinated classroom and clinical experiences during the junior and senior years. Schools that offer the program (see Appendix C) must follow specific guidelines for program assessment, development, implementation, and evaluation. Each must also meet prescribed standards for organization and administration, faculty and staff, facilities, and student services.

In contrast to the didactic program, the clinical component for the coordinated undergraduate program is supervised by college or university faculty members and consists of a minimum of nine hundred hours. In the coordinated program, the need for an internship after graduation is eliminated. Thus, it takes five years to become professionally qualified in the didactic program, but only four years in this program.

Pre-Professional Practice Programs (AP4)

The pre-professional practice program provides a minimum of nine hundred hours of supervised practice. Programs follow completion of at least a baccalaureate degree and didactic academic requirements. Some programs may be part-time, with supervised practice at a minimum of twenty hours per week and completed within a two-year period. This program replaces the six- to twelve-month work experience previously allowed (see Appendix E).

All programs are in compliance with the standards of education. Program graduates who are verified by the program director are eligible to apply for active membership in the American Dietetic Association and/or to take the registration examination.

Registration Examination

Completion of the registration examination for dietitians is required to receive R.D. status. One must complete the previously listed educational requirements to be eligible to take the R.D. exam. Currently the exam is in a computerized format and is provided by numerous test centers nationwide. The advantages of the computerized format are: decreased testing time, increased testing precision, immediate feedback to the candidate, on-demand testing schedule where test takers can schedule an appointment with the testing center whenever they are ready to take the test, and quicker retesting availability.[2]

The R.D. exam consists of a range of 125 to 145 test questions that cover all aspects of the profession. To prepare for the exam it is important to use some strategy, including:

- The review of course texts and/or notes
- A study group
- Formal review courses, either on-site or self-study
- Commission on Dietetic Registration (CDR) study guide
- Self-made or professionally developed flashcards

For information on the R.D. exam implementation and administration, contact the Commission on Dietetic Registration (CDR) at cdrnet.org. Refer to the back of the *Journal of the American Dietetic Association* for listings of formal review courses.

Advanced Specialty

To recognize advanced-level practice, specialty competence certification is now available. The Commission on Dietetic Registration administers a program to recognize specialists in distinct practice disciplines. To be certified as a "specialist practitioner," individuals applying for this designation must meet certain eligibility criteria and successfully complete either an examination or a portfolio assessment.[3]

A Changing Climate

As dietetic leaders project the future education of dietitians, graduates of education programs must be prepared to perform the expected functions of the dietetic practitioner in a dramatically changing system. More than ever before, education must be made relevant to practice.

It is important for students to develop an education program that will meet their individual needs and practice interests. More specifically, the student should be aware of the areas in education that should be strengthened based on current practice demand. These include: a broader base, particularly in arts, humanities, and behavioral sciences; a greater emphasis on management and business; a greater emphasis on communications and networking; a greater emphasis on computer technology; a greater depth in scientific knowledge of nutrition; and a greater knowledge about food and cooking.

It is apparent that education must meet the individual's needs and specialty interests. Open course work should focus on those areas that the students perceive as being important to their practice in the field. In addition, students should seek volunteer work through hospitals, restaurants, resorts and spas, outpatient facilities, nursing homes, schools, and so forth. This will enable them to develop field experience to help determine realistic career objectives.

Dietitians of the future will not be able to serve as leaders unless the rigor and the credibility of their educational experiences are strengthened. The same is true for basic education programs, field experiences, advanced education in specialty areas, on-the-job training, graduate programs leading to advanced degrees, and continuing education.

Educational requirements in the field are under constant review and are subject to change. For the most up-to-date information, contact:

The American Dietetic Association
216 West Jackson Boulevard, Suite 800
Chicago, IL 60606-6995
eatright.org

11

DESIGN FOR TOMORROW

THE SUBJECT OF nutrition has never been as popular as it is now. The general public is increasing its interest in health from a wellness standpoint. These facts help create a positive environment for the practice of dietetics.

However, the practice environment is changing. Dietitians willing to change and grow, to study hard, to keep up-to-date, and to choose the profession as a lifelong career will find that the challenges can be met and a bright future is possible.

The Changing Scene

Six factors influence the demand for dietetic services. These include (1) socioeconomic trends; (2) public policy; (3) health values, attitudes, and behaviors; (4) technological advances; (5) competition; and (6) changes in the profession.

Social and economic trends are influenced by:

- Population demographics, which affect the supply of professionals, the needs for goods and services, and the location of clients
- The economic climate, which affects public funding for nutrition programs, the ability of clients to pay for the services, food pricing, and the supply of professionals
- Health expenditures, which affect available dollars for preventive services and reimbursement policies

Public policy is influenced by:

- The existence of publicly supported nutrition programs
- The degree of regulatory control
- Reimbursement schedules
- Wage guidelines

Health values, attitudes, and behaviors are influenced by:

- The population's attitudes toward nutrition services and care
- Consumer-oriented decisions regarding health care
- Payment for nutrition services

Technological advances influence:

- The delivery of food and services
- The use of communication resources and computer applications
- Creation of new dietetic roles

Competition influences:

- The consumers' ability to seek the dietitian for nutrition care
- The fees for services and the payment system

Changes in the profession influence:

- The visibility of the dietitian
- The supply of dietitians
- The demand for nutrition services

The influence of these six areas will continue to change practice environments and expand the nutrition services required by industry, government, the medical profession, and the general public.

The direction of the future demand for dietitians based on the previously listed influences on the profession is illustrated in the following chart, which represents the optimal scenario for future demand based on employer type.

Employer	Optimal Scenario
Nongovernment Organizations	
Health care facilities/organizations	Increase
Educational institutions	No change
Commercial	Increase
Other (church, nonprofit, and so forth)	No change
Food-service operations	Increase
Corporate health facilities	Increase
Self-employed or partnership dietitians or other health providers (M.D., D.M.D., and so forth)	Increase

Dietitians in nontraditional fields (cooking schools, restaurants, public relations, product development)	Increase

Governmental Organizations

City or county government health care facilities/organizations	Increase
Educational institutions	No change
State government health care facilities/ organizations	Increase
Educational institutions	No change
Federal government health care facilities/ organizations	Increase
Educational institutions	No change

This scenario contains a mixture of positive and negative elements. Fewer registered dietitians will be employed in hospitals, in higher education, and by government; more will have jobs in business and industry, consulting practices, and noninstitutional health care facilities.

What impact will this changing scenario have on dietetic practice? The nutrition professional may need to focus on future progress in the following areas:

- Professional education
- Research
- Marketing of nutrition services
- Cost-effective health care
- International dietetics

Education

New competencies or enhancement of current competencies will be demanded as dietitians move into advanced levels of practice. Professionals in many fields are finding it necessary to add additional knowledge and skills to their basic competencies to make themselves more marketable; dietetic professionals are no exception. The only way other professionals will recognize a dietitian's expertise is for the dietitian to demonstrate that she or he has the knowledge and the competencies in many skill areas to perform required tasks. Dietitians are going back to college to learn pharmacy, exercise physiology, biochemistry, culinary skills, communications, and business skills, among others.[1]

For the clinical dietitian specialist, the need will be for additional competency in biochemistry, physiology, pharmacology, management (including cost/benefit analysis), nutritional care computer applications, leadership skills to influence legislation in the political arena, and professional assertiveness. Also, clinical nutrition is moving out of the hospital and into communities, especially retirement and assisted-living communities. Knowledge and skills are needed to provide nutritional care services for this aging population. As well, the rising incidences of diabetes and other obesity-related problems will increase the services of clinical dietitians in the offices and clinics of physicians.

For the administrative dietitian, the need will be for competencies in cost/benefit analysis, food-service management computer applications, cooperative group purchasing, enhanced writing skills for technical and administrative reports, and leadership skills to influence legislation in the political arena. Government initiatives and trends will need to be tracked. These areas include food security and safety, food assistance and feeding programs, protection from bioterrorism, and food and nutrition research.

For the community dietitian, the need will be for increased emphasis on leadership for wellness programs and lifestyle-change clinics and programs, an understanding of the cultural values and food habits of ethnic groups, and the skills needed for writing grant proposals. There is an increased demand for nutritional counseling in schools, prisons, community health programs, and home health care agencies. In addition, dietitians will enter the home through the Internet, home visiting, outpatient clinic services, advice hotlines, and through other means.

Research

Research is becoming an essential component to document the value of nutrition services and for achieving third-party payment for services provided. Therefore, it is essential for the dietetic practitioner to develop consistent care, based on standardized protocols or criteria that have been developed for quality assurance.

Clinical, community, and administrative dietitians must be able to justify their services by documentation of both process and outcome. They should be able to clearly demonstrate that a positive change in diet will reduce risk factors, which in turn will lead to better health and economic savings. Therefore, the desired outcome of research will be to demonstrate clearly that nutrition services contribute to the quality of life and can be provided cost-effectively.

Marketing

Many consumers are not informed about the nutrition services available to them or about dietitians who are qualified to provide the services. Individuals depend upon physicians and other allied health professionals—who are often not very knowledgeable about what dietitians do—to advise them about health and nutrition services. Dietetics has to be relevant to more people, in more circumstances, at more life stages, and in more cultures. This means developing ways in which the dietary message can be understood across cultures and in everyone's home.

The dietitian must, therefore, apply marketing strategies to inform the public and other health care providers about the nutrition services available and to inform them that the dietitian is the professional educated to provide these nutrition services. The public will need continued information on new food choices, along with advice on how to prepare and use new foods. As foods are chosen or engineered to more closely fit particular people's needs, the work of registered dietitians could become more complex but ultimately more valued. Consider the differences in dietary needs of a nine-year-old burn victim, a fifty-five-year-old with a family history of Alzheimer's, and a marathon cyclist. Their differing needs are a far cry from a one-size-fits-all approach.

Target groups of this marketing effort should include the general public, third-party payers, specific employer and employee groups, and public policy makers. In addition, the current emphasis on health will increase the roles of the dietitian and will expand marketing of professional services, especially in preventive counseling to industry and to the public directly.

Provision of Cost-Effective Health Care

Predictions for health care, in general, indicate a continued growth of alternate delivery systems, such as health maintenance organizations (HMOs). Services traditionally provided in hospitals will continue to be converted to out-of-hospital care by provision of lower levels of care in skilled nursing facilities and home health care. Corporate control of health care will continue to grow. Support of employers for employee health promotion will continue through growing numbers of wellness programs. Consumers are becoming very cost conscious and will seek quality services at a reasonable cost.

The nature of these changes taking place in health care is so fundamental as to present a threat to those who fail to respond and an opportunity to those who take action promptly.

Action by dietetic practitioners is the key. There is a need again to market nutrition services to the general public, employer/employee groups, third-party payers, prepaid health plans, and national and state public policy formulators. Dietitians must demonstrate the value of their services by documenting the cost and the effectiveness of services.

The American Dietetic Association

The American Dietetic Association provides a means for the dietetic profession to identify those issues that must be addressed, to set goals that need to be accomplished, and to conduct programs that will strengthen the ability of dietitians to meet the needs of society. In doing so, the association supports the profession by enabling members to work together to achieve vital goals that are unattainable by individual efforts.

In addition, the association provides essential communication for members via:

- Publication of the *Journal of the American Dietetic Association*
- Information on topics ranging from legislation to public relations, dietetic education, and others

- Data and information about specific areas of practice
- State ADA associations
- Internet access at eatright.org
- National convention held every October

The challenge to catch up, keep up, and get ahead has become a joint responsibility. Dietitians working with the American Dietetic Association through dietetic practice groups and state and district associations have the opportunity to transform this field into a cutting-edge profession that addresses emerging and evolving needs of American society.

International Dietetics

International food and nutrition issues in both developed and developing nations around the world continue to grow and change. Dietetics professionals will collect and use evidence to improve the effectiveness of nutrition therapy to reduce acute and chronic diseases. In addition, the human immunodeficiency virus, aging, biotechnology, and food safety issues are of concern.

The American Dietetics Association and the Dietitians of Canada are joining forces to focus on international issues through print materials, the release of joint public policy, and continuing education events. Each member has a role to play in this international market, whether it is associated with personal learning related to a new culture and its indigenous foods, participating in national programs that contribute to the world's knowledge and information, or realizing the importance of sharing within the international community. Each dietetics professional is an example of nutrition "in action" in some part of the world.[2]

Appendix A

Associations

National

American Celiac Society/Dietary Support Coalition
58 Musano Ct.
West Orange, NJ 07052-4114
ddnc.org

American College of Nutrition
Hospital for Joint Diseases
301 E. 17th St.
New York, NY 10003
am-coll-nutr.org

American Dietetic Association
216 W. Jackson Blvd., Ste. 800
Chicago, IL 60606
eatright.org

American Society for Clinical Nutrition
9650 Rockville Pike
Bethesda, MD 20814
faseb.org/ascn

American Society for Nutritional Sciences
9650 Rockville Pike
Bethesda, MD 20814
asns.org

American Society for Parenteral and Enteral Nutrition
8630 Fenton St., Ste. 412
Silver Spring, MD 20910-3805
nutritioncare.org

Association of Vegetarian Dietitians and Nutrition Educators
3835 State Route 414
Burdett, NY 14818

Child Nutrition Forum
1875 Connecticut Ave. NW, Ste. 540
Washington, DC 20009
frac.org

Consultant Dietitians in Health Care Facilities
216 W. Jackson Blvd., Ste. 800
Chicago, II 60606

Dietary Managers Association
406 Surrey Woods Dr.
St. Charles, IL 60174
dmaonline.org

Nutrition Screening Initiative
1010 Wisconsin Ave. NW, Ste. 800
Washington, DC 20007

International

American Overseas Dietetic Association
Joseph-Greissing-Strasse 8
74523 Schwaebisch Hall
Germany
49/791-49-0021
eatrightoverseas.org

Dietitians of Canada
601-480 University Ave., Ste. 604
Toronto, ON
Canada M5G 1V2
dietitians.ca

Puerto Rico Chapter of ADA
P.O. Box 360915
San Juan, PR 00936-0915

State ADA Affiliate Associations

Alabama Dietetic Association
P.O. Box 11594
Montgomery, AL 36111-0594
eatrightalabama.org

Alaska Dietetic Association
P.O. Box 2627
Bethel, AK 99559-2627
eatrightalaska.org

Arizona Dietetic Association
P.O. Box 10344
Phoenix, AZ 85064
eatrightarizona.org

Arkansas Dietetic Association
P.O. Box 55234
Little Rock, AR 72215-5234
arkansaseatright.org

California Dietetic Association
7740 Manchester Ave., Ste. 102
Plaza del Rey, CA 90293-8499
dietitian.org

Colorado Dietetic Association
1301 Pennsylvania St., Ste. 250
Denver, CO 80203
eatrightcolorado.org

Connecticut Dietetic Association
18 Sakrison Rd.
Granby, CT 06035
eatrightct.org

Delaware Dietetic Association
232 Steeplechase Circle
Wilmington, DE 19808
dedietassn.org

District of Columbia
DC Hospital Association
1250 I St. NW, #700
Washington, DC 20005-3922
dcmada.org

Florida Dietetic Association
P.O. Box 12608
Tallahassee, FL 32317-2608
eatrightflorida.org

Georgia Dietetic Association
1260 Winchester Pkwy., Ste. 205
Smyrna, GA 30080
gda-online.org

Hawaii Dietetic Association
248 Aumoe Rd.
Kailua, HI 96734-3444
nutritionhawaii.org

Idaho Dietetic Association
306 Oregon St.
Gooding, ID 83330-1442
eatrightidaho.org

Illinois Dietetic Association
P.O. Box 26
70 S. Richard St.
Henry, IL 61537
eatrightillinois.org

Indiana Dietetic Association
150 N. Illinois St.
Elberfeld, IN 47613
dietetics.com/ida

Iowa Dietetic Association
27924 Butler Center Rd.
Clarksville, IA 50619
eatrightiowa.org

Kansas Dietetic Association
3133 U. Ave.
Herrington, KS 67449-5027
dietetics.com/kda

Kentucky Dietetic Association
P.O. Box 23555
Lexington, KY 40523-3555
kyeatright.org

Louisiana Dietetic Association
8550 United Plaza Blvd., Ste. 1001
Baton Rouge, LA 70809
eatrightlda.org

Maine Dietetic Association
96 Waterman Dr.
New Gloucester, ME 04260-3062
eatrightmaine.org

Maryland Dietetic Association
11319 Glen Arm Rd.
Glen Arm, MD 21057-9434
eatwellmd.org

Massachusetts Dietetic Association
P.O. Box 66812
Falmouth, MA 04105
massnutrition.org

Michigan Dietetic Association
3319 Greenfield Rd., #321
Dearborn, MI 48120
eatrightmich.org

Minnesota Dietetic Association
1910 W. Country Road B, Ste. 212
St. Paul, MN 55113-5448
mndietetics.org

Mississippi Dietetic Association
330 N. Mart Plaza
Jackson, MS 39206
eatrightmississippi.org

Missouri Dietetic Association
P.O. Box 1225
Jefferson City, MO 65102-1225
eatrightmissouri.org

Montana Dietetic Association
1733 E. Broadway St.
Helena, MT 59601-4609
montanadieteticassociation.org

Nebraska Dietetic Association
103 S. Michigan Ave.
York, NE 68467-4617
eatrightnebraska.org

Nevada Dietetic Association
University of Nevada School of Medicine
Mail Stop 333
Reno, NV 89557
nevadard.org

New Hampshire Dietetic Association
28 Stevens Hill Rd.
Nottingham, NH 03290-4801
eatrightnh.org

New Jersey Dietetic Association
1 AAA Dr., Ste. 102
Trenton, NJ 08691
eatrightnj.org

New Mexico Dietetic Association
2301 Aguacate Dr. NW
Albuquerque, NM 87120-2858

New York State Dietetic Association
P.O. Box 30953
New York, NY 10011-0109
eatrightny.org

North Carolina Dietetic Association
1500 Sunday Dr., Ste. 102
Raleigh, NC 27607-5163
eatrightnc.org

North Dakota Dietetic Association
2603 Olive St.
Grand Forks, ND 58201
eatrightnd.org

Ohio Dietetic Association
5310 E. Main St., Ste. 104
Columbus, OH 43213
eatrightohio.org

Oklahoma Dietetic Association
125 HES
Stillwater, OK 74078-6116
oknutrition.org

Oregon Dietetic Association
5811 SE Salmon St.
Portland, OR 97215-2738
eatrightoregon.org

Pennsylvania Dietetic Association
P.O. Box 60870
Harrisburg, PA 17106-0870
eatrightpa.org

Rhode Island Dietetic Association
P.O. Box 6892
Providence, RI 02904-6892
eatrightri.org

South Carolina Dietetic Association
P.O. Box 1763
Columbia, SC 29202
eatrightsc.org

South Dakota Dietetic Association
25414 483rd Ave.
Garretson, SD 57030
sdaho.org/sddapage.htm

Tennessee Dietetic Association
2706 Greystone Rd.
Nashville, TN 37204
eatright-tn.org

Texas Dietetic Association
12300 Ford Rd., Ste. 135
Dallas, TX 75234
nutrition4texas.org

Utah Dietetic Association
2072 N. 50 West
Layton, UT 84041
eatrightutah.org

Vermont Dietetic Association
P.O. Box 112
Saint Johnsbury, VT 05819
eatrightvt.org

Virginia Dietetic Association
P.O. Box 439
Centerville, VA 20122
eatright-va.org

Washington State Dietetic Association
P.O. Box 46998
Seattle, WA 98146
nutritionwsda.org

West Virginia Dietetic Association
Marshall University
Department of Dietetics
1 John Marshall Dr.
Huntington, WV 25755-0001
wvda.org

Wisconsin Dietetic Association
1411 W. Montgomery St.
Sparta, WI 54656-1003
eatrightwisc.org

Wyoming Dietetic Association
Department of Family and Consumer Science
P.O. Box 3354
Laramie, WY 82071
wyomingdieteticassociation.org

For more information, go to http://eatright.org. In addition, many of the state affiliates have job listing sites.

Appendix B

Didactic Programs

Didactic Program in Dietetics (DPD) is a phrase used by the American Dietetic Association to describe the program approved under the standards of education as meeting course work requirements culminating in at least a bachelor's degree.

Each of the following programs is approved by the Commission on Accreditation/Approval for Dietetics Education. Graduates of these programs who are verified by the program director may apply for dietetic internships or pre-professional practice programs to establish eligibility for membership in the American Dietetic Association.

Alabama

Auburn University
Department of Nutrition and Food Science
328 Spidle Hall
Auburn, AL 36849-5605
auburn.edu

Samford University
Department of Human Sciences and Design
800 Lakeshore Dr.
Birmingham, AL 35229-2239
samford.edu

Oakwood College
Family and Consumer Sciences
Huntsville, AL 35896
oakwood.edu

Jacksonville State University
Department of Family and Consumer Sciences
Mason Hall
Jacksonville, AL 36265
jsu.edu

University of Montevallo
Department of Family and Consumer Sciences
Station #6385
Montevallo, AL 35115-6000
montevallo.edu

Alabama A&M University
Area of Nutrition and Hospitality Management
Box 639
Normal, AL 35762
aamu.edu

University of Alabama
Department of Human Nutrition and Hospitality Management
Box 870158
Tuscaloosa, AL 35487-0158
ua.edu

Tuskegee University
Department of Home Economics
202 Washington Hall
Tuskegee, AL 36088
tuskegee.edu

Arizona

Northern Arizona University
Food and Nutrition Science
NAU Box 15095
Flagstaff, AZ 86011-5095
nau.edu

Arizona State University
Department of Family Resources and Human Development
Box 872502
Tempe, AZ 85287-2502
asu.edu

University of Arizona
Department of Nutritional Sciences
Tucson, AZ 85721
arizona.edu

Arkansas

Ouachita Baptist University
Department of Family and Consumer Sciences
P.O. Box 3769
Arkadelphia, AR 71998-0001
obu.edu

University of Central Arkansas
Department of Family and Consumer Sciences
McAlister Hall 100
Conway, AR 72035-0001
uca.edu

University of Arkansas
School of Human Environmental Sciences
118 HOEC
Fayetteville, AR 72701
uark.edu

University of Arkansas at Pine Bluff
Department of Human Services
P.O. Box 4971
Pine Bluff, AR 71611
uapb.edu

Harding University
Department of Family and Consumer Sciences
Box 12233
900 E. Center Ave.
Searcy, AR 72149-0001
harding.edu

California

Pacific Union College
Family and Consumer Sciences Department
Angwin, CA 94508-9797
puc.edu

University of California, Berkeley
Department of Nutritional Sciences
119 Morgan Hall
Berkeley, CA 94720-3104
berkeley.edu

California State University, Chico
Department of Biological Science
Tehama Hall, 124
Chico, CA 95929-0002
csuchico.edu

University of California, Davis
Department of Nutrition
3143 Meyer Hall
Davis, CA 95616-8669
ucdavis.edu

California State University, Fresno
Department of Enology, Food Science, and Nutrition
5300 N. Campus Dr.
Fresno, CA 93740-0017
csufresno.edu

California State University, Long Beach
Department of Family and Consumer Sciences
1250 Bellflower Blvd.
Long Beach, CA 90840-0501
csulb.edu

California State University, Los Angeles
Department of Health and Nutritional Sciences
5151 State University Dr.
Los Angeles, CA 90032-8172
calstatela.edu

Pepperdine University
Natural Science Division
Malibu, CA 90263
pepperdine.edu

California State University, Northridge
Department of Family Environmental Sciences
18111 Nordhoff St.
Northridge, CA 91330-8308
csun.edu

California State Polytechnic University
Nutrition and Consumer Sciences
3801 W. Temple Ave.
Pomona, CA 91768
csupomona.edu

California State University, Sacramento
Department of Human Environmental Sciences
6000 J St.
Sacramento, CA 95819-6053
csus.edu

California State University, San Bernardino
Department of Health Science & Human Ecology
5500 University Pkwy.
San Bernardino, CA 92407-2397
csusb.edu

San Diego State University
Department of Exercise and Nutritional Sciences
San Diego, CA 92182-0171
sdsu.edu

San Francisco State University
Consumer and Family Studies/Dietetics
1600 Holloway
San Francisco, CA 94132
sfsu.edu

San Jose State University
Department of Nutrition and Food Science
San Jose, CA 95192-0058
sjsu.edu

Colorado

Colorado State University
Department of Food Science and Human Nutrition
Fort Collins, CO 80523-1571
colostate.edu

University of Northern Colorado
Department of Community Health and Nutrition
Gunter 2320
Greeley, CO 80639
univnorthco.edu

Connecticut

University of Connecticut
Department of Nutritional Sciences
3624 Horsebarn Rd. Extension
Storrs, CT 06269
uconn.edu

St. Joseph College
Department of Nutrition and Family Studies
1678 Asylum Ave.
West Hartford, CT 06117
sjc.edu

University of New Haven
School of Hotel/Restaurant/Dietetics and Tourism Administration
Department of Dietetics
300 Orange Ave.
West Haven, CT 06516
newhaven.edu

Delaware

Delaware State University
Department of Family and Consumer Sciences
1200 N. Dupont Hwy.
Dover, DE 19901-2277
dsc.edu

University of Delaware
Department of Nutrition and Dietetics
234A Alison Hall
Newark, DE 19716-3301
udel.edu

District of Columbia

University of the District of Columbia
Department of Biological and Environmental Sciences
4200 Connecticut Ave. NW
Bldg. 44, Rm. 200-02
Washington, DC 20008
udc.edu

Florida

University of Florida
Food Science and Human Nutrition Department
359 FSB
Gainesville, FL 32611
ufl.edu

University of North Florida
College of Health
4567 St. Johns Bluff Rd. South
Jacksonville, FL 32224-2645
unf.edu

Florida International University
Department of Dietetics and Nutrition
HB 208 University Park
Miami, FL 33199
fiu.edu

Florida State University
Department of Nutrition, Food, and Movement Sciences
College of Human Sciences
Tallahassee, FL 32306-1493
fsu.edu

Georgia

University of Georgia
Department of Food and Nutrition
College of Family and Consumer Sciences
Dawson Hall
Athens, GA 30602
uga.edu

Georgia State University
Department of Nutrition
Box 873
University Plaza
Atlanta, GA 30303-3083
gsu.edu

Fort Valley State College
Department of Family and Consumer Sciences
805 State College Dr.
Fort Valley, GA 31030
fvsu.edu

Life College
Department of Nutrition
1269 Barclay Circle
Marietta, GA 30060
life.edu

Georgia Southern University
Department of Family and Consumer Sciences
Box 8034
Statesboro, GA 30460-8034
gasou.edu

Hawaii

University of Hawaii-Manoa
Department of Food Science and Human Nutrition
2515 Campus Rd.
Miller Hall 12B
Honolulu, HI 96822
hawaii.edu

Idaho

Idaho State University
Department of Health and Nutrition Sciences
Box 8109
Pocatello, ID 83209-8109
isu.edu

Illinois

Southern Illinois University at Carbondale
Department of Animal Science, Food, and Nutrition
Mailcode 4317
Carbondale, IL 62901-4317
siu.edu

Eastern Illinois University
School of Family and Consumer Sciences
600 Lincoln Ave.
Charleston, IL 61920-3099
eiu.edu

Loyola University Chicago
Department of Food and Nutrition
6525 N. Sheridan Rd.
Chicago, IL 60626
luc.edu

Northern Illinois University
School of Family, Consumer, and Nutrition Sciences
DeKalb, IL 60115-2854
niu.edu

Olivet Nazarene University
Department of Family and Consumer Science
P.O. Box 592
Kankakee, IL 60901-0592
olivet.edu

Benedictine University
Department of Biological Sciences
5700 College Rd.
Lisle, IL 60532-0900
ben.edu

Western Illinois University
Department of Family and Consumer Sciences
Macomb, IL 61455-1396
wiu.edu

Illinois State University
Family and Consumer Sciences
Campus Box 5060
Normal, IL 61790-5060
ilstu.edu

Bradley University
Family and Consumer Sciences Department
1501 W. Bradley Ave.
Peoria, IL 61625
bradley.edu

Dominican University
Department of Nutrition Sciences
7900 W. Division St.
River Forest, IL 60305
dom.edu

University of Illinois
Department of Food Science and Human Nutrition
345 Bevier Hall
905 S. Goodwin Ave.
Urbana, IL 61801
uiuc.edu

Indiana

Indiana University
Department of Applied Health Science
HPER 116
Bloomington, IN 47405-4801
iub.edu

Marian College
Department of Nursing and Nutrition Sciences
Food and Nutrition Sciences Program
3200 Cold Springs Rd.
Indianapolis, IN 46222-1997
marian.edu

Ball State University
Department of Family and Consumer Sciences
Muncie, IN 47306-0250
bsu.edu

Purdue University
Department of Foods and Nutrition
1264 Stone Hall
West Lafayette, IN 47907-1264
purdue.edu

Iowa

Iowa State University
Department of Food Science and Human Nutrition
1104 Human Nutrition Center
Ames, IA 50011-1120
iastate.edu

University of Northern Iowa
Department of Design, Family, and Consumer Sciences
235 Latham Hall
Cedar Falls, IA 50614-0332
uni.edu

Kansas

Kansas State University
Department of Hotel, Restaurant, Institution Management,
   and Dietetics
Department of Food and Nutrition
Justin Hall 103
Manhattan, KS 66506-1404
ksu.edu

Kentucky

Berea College
Department of Child and Family Studies
C.P.O. 2319
Berea, KY 40404
berea.edu

Western Kentucky University
Department of Consumer and Family Sciences
Academic Complex 302F
One Big Red Way
Bowling Green, KY 42101-3576
wku.edu

University of Kentucky
College of Human Environmental Sciences
Department of Nutrition and Food Science
218 Funkhouser Bldg.
Lexington, KY 40506-0054
uky.edu

Morehead State University
Department of Home Economics
P.O. 889
Morehead, KY 40351-1689
morehead-st.edu

Murray State University
Department of Family and Consumer Studies
Murray, KY 42071-0009
mursuky.edu

Eastern Kentucky University
Home Economics Department
102 Burrier
Richmond, KY 40475-3107
eku.edu

Louisiana

Louisiana State University
School of Human Ecology
Baton Rouge, LA 70803-4300
lsu.edu

Southern University
College of Agriculture and Home Economics
Department of Human Nutrition and Food
P.O. Box 11342
Baton Rouge, LA 70813
subr.edu

University of Southwestern Louisiana
College of Applied Life Sciences
School of Human Resources
P.O. Box 40399
Lafayette, LA 70504
louisiana.edu

McNeese State University
P.O. Box 92820
Lake Charles, LA 70609-2820
mcneese.edu

Louisiana Tech University
School of Human Ecology
P.O. Box 3167
Ruston, LA 71272
latech.edu

Nicholls State University
Department of Family and Consumer Sciences
Box 2014
Thibodaux, LA 70310
nicholls.edu

Maine

University of Maine
Department of Food Science and Human Nutrition
5749 Merrill Hall, Rm. 27
Orono, ME 04469-5749
umaine.edu

Maryland

Morgan State University
Department of Human Ecology
Key Building #152
Coldspring La. and Hillen Rd.
Baltimore, MD 21239-4098
morgan.edu

University of Maryland
Department of Nutrition and Food Science
College Park, MD 20742-7521
umd.edu

University of Maryland, Eastern Shore
Department of Human Ecology
Princess Anne, MD 21853-1299
umes.edu

Massachusetts

University of Massachusetts
Department of Nutrition, Box 31420
Chenoweth Laboratory
Amherst, MA 01003-1420
umass.edu

Simmons College
Department of Nutrition
300 The Fenway
Boston, MA 02115-5898
simmons.edu

Framingham State College
Family and Consumer Sciences Department
100 State St.
Framingham, MA 01701-9101
framingham.edu

Michigan

University of Michigan
School of Public Health
Human Nutrition Program
1420 Washington Heights
Ann Arbor, MI 48109-2029
umich.edu
(Bachelor's degree prerequisite for admission)

Andrews University
Department of Nutrition
Berrien Springs, MI 49104-0210
andrews.edu

Marygrove College
Human Ecology Department
8425 W. McNichols Rd.
Detroit, MI 48221-2599
marygrove.edu

Michigan State University
Department of Food Science and Human Nutrition
2112 Anthony Hall
East Lansing, MI 48824-1030
msu.edu

Western Michigan University
Department of Family and Consumer Sciences
3024 Kohrman Hall
Kalamazoo, MI 49008
wmich.edu

Madonna University
Department of Biological and Health Sciences
36600 Schoolcraft Rd.
Livonia, MI 48150-1173
munet.edu

Northern Michigan University
HPER
Marquette, MI 49855
nmu.edu

Central Michigan University
Human Environmental Studies
Wightman Hall 205
Mt. Pleasant, MI 48859
cmich.edu

Minnesota

The College of St. Scholastica
Department of Dietetics
1200 Kenwood Ave.
Duluth, MN 55811-4199
css.edu

Mankato State University
Family Consumer Science Department
MSU 44, P.O. Box 8400
Mankato, MN 56002-8400
mnsu.edu

Concordia College
Department of Family and Nutrition Sciences
Moorhead, MN 56562
cord.edu

College of St. Catherine
Family Consumer and Nutritional Sciences
2004 Randolph Ave.
St. Paul, MN 55105
stkate.edu

University of Minnesota
Department of Food Science and Nutrition
1334 Eckles Ave.
St. Paul, MN 55108-6099
umn.edu

Mississippi

University of Southern Mississippi
School of Home Economics
Box 5035
Hattiesburg, MS 39406-5035
usm.edu

Alcorn State University
Department of Family and Consumer Sciences
1000 ASU Dr. #839
Lorman, MS 39096-9402
alcorn.edu

Mississippi State University
School of Human Sciences
Box 9746
Mississippi State, MS 39762-9746
msstate.edu

University of Mississippi
Department of Family and Consumer Sciences
Meek Hall
University, MS 38677
olemiss.edu

Missouri

Southeast Missouri State University
Department of Human Environmental Studies
Cape Girardeau, MO 63701-4799
semo.edu

Northwest Missouri State University
College of Education and Human Services
Department of Human Environmental Sciences
Administration Bldg., Rm. 309
Maryville, MO 64468-6001
nwmissouri.edu

College of the Ozarks
Dietetics and Nutrition Education
Point Lookout, MO 65726
ozarks.edu

Southwest Missouri State University
Department of Biomedical Sciences
Springfield, MO 65804
smsu.edu

Fontbonne University
Department of Human Environmental Sciences
6800 Wydown Blvd.
St. Louis, MO 63105-3098
fontbonne.edu

St. Louis University
School of Allied Health Professions
Department of Nutrition and Dietetics
3437 Caroline St.
St. Louis, MO 63104-1111
slu.edu

Central Missouri State University
Department of Human Environmental Sciences
Warrensburg, MO 64093-5022
cmsu.edu

Montana

Montana State University
Department of Health and Human Development
201 Romney
Bozeman, MT 59717-0336
montana.edu

Nebraska

University of Nebraska, Kearney
Department of Family and Consumer Sciences
Otto Olsen Bldg., Rm. 205C
Kearney, NE 68849-2130
unk.edu

University of Nebraska, Lincoln
Department of Nutritional Science and Dietetics
202 Ruth Leverton Hall
Lincoln, NE 68583-0806
unl.edu

Nevada

University of Nevada, Reno
Department of Nutrition
Mail Stop 142
Reno, NV 89557-0132
unr.edu

New Hampshire

University of New Hampshire
Human Nutrition Center, Colovos Rd.
Durham, NH 03824
unh.edu

Keene State College
Home Economics/Human Services
Joslin House, Rm. 207
Keene, NH 03435-2903
keene.edu

New Jersey

College of St. Elizabeth
Department of Foods and Nutrition
2 Convent Rd.
Morristown, NJ 07960-6989
cse.edu

Rutgers University
Department of Nutritional Sciences
Davison Hall
26 Nichol Ave.
New Brunswick, NJ 08901-2882
rutgers.edu

Montclair State University
Department of Human Ecology
Upper Montclair, NJ 07043
montclair.edu

New Mexico

University of New Mexico
Nutrition/Dietetics Program
Division of Individual, Family, and Community Education
Albuquerque, NM 87131-1231
unm.edu

New Mexico State University
Department of Family and Consumer Sciences
Box 30003/MSC 3470
Las Cruces, NM 88003-8003
nmsu.edu

New York

Herbert H. Lehman College
Department of Health Services, Dietetics, Food, and Nutrition
Bedford Park Blvd. West
Bronx, NY 10468-1589
lehman.cuny.edu

Brooklyn College
Department of Health and Nutrition Sciences
2900 Bedford Ave.
Brooklyn, NY 11210-2889
brooklyn.cuny.edu

Long Island University/C.W. Post Campus
Health Science Department
720 Northern Blvd.
Brookville, NY 11548
liunet.edu

State University College at Buffalo
Nutrition, Hospitality, and Fashion Department
1300 Elmwood Ave.
Buffalo, NY 14222-1095
buffalo.edu

Queens College
Department of Family, Nutrition, and Exercise Sciences
65-30 Kissena Blvd.
Flushing, NY 11367-1597
qc.edu

Cornell University, Ithaca
Division of Nutritional Sciences
3M5 Martha Van Rensselaer Hall
Ithaca, NY 14853-4401
cornell.edu

Cornell University, Ithaca
School of Hotel Administration
252 Statler Hall
Ithaca, NY 14853-6962
hotelschool.cornell.edu

Hunter College, City University of New York
School of Health Sciences
Brookdale Health Science Center
425 E. Twenty-Fifth St.
New York, NY 10010-2590
hunter.cuny.edu

New York University
Department of Nutrition and Food Studies
35 W. Fourth St., 10th Fl.
New York, NY 10012-1172
nyu.edu

State University of New York at Oneonta
Department of Human Ecology
Oneonta, NY 13820-4015
oneonta.edu

Plattsburgh State University of New York
Nursing, Food, and Nutrition
101 Broad St.
Plattsburgh, NY 12901-2681
plattsburgh.edu

Rochester Institute of Technology
School of Food, Hotel, and Travel Management
One Lomb Memorial Dr.
Rochester, NY 14623-5604
rit.edu

Syracuse University
Department of Nutrition and Food-Service Management
034 Slocum Hall
Syracuse, NY 13244-1250
syr.edu

Marymount College
Department of Human Ecology
Marian Hall
Tarrytown, NY 10591-3796
marymt.edu

Russell Sage College
Nutrition Science Program
Ackerman Hall
Troy, NY 12180-4115
sage.edu

North Carolina

Appalachian State University
Department of Family and Consumer Sciences
Boone, NC 28608
appstate.edu

University of North Carolina, Chapel Hill
Department of Nutrition
McGavran-Greenberg Hall
CB #7400
Chapel Hill, NC 27599-7400
unc.edu

Western Carolina University
Department of Health Sciences
Cullowhee, NC 28723-9054
wcu.edu

North Carolina Central University
Department of Human Sciences
P.O. Box 19615
Durham, NC 27707
nccu.edu

Bennett College
Home Economics Department
900 E. Washington St.
Greensboro, NC 27401-3239
bennett.edu

North Carolina A&T State University
Department of Home Economics
105 Benbrow Hall
Greensboro, NC 27411-1064

University of North Carolina at Greensboro
Nutrition and Food-Service Systems
P.O. Box 26170
Greensboro, NC 27402-6170
uncg.edu

East Carolina University
School of Human Environmental Sciences
Department of Nutrition and Hospitality Management
Greenville, NC 27858-4353
ecu.edu

Meredith College
Department of Human Environmental Sciences
Foods and Nutrition
3800 Hillsborough St.
Raleigh, NC 27607-5298
meredith.edu

North Dakota

North Dakota State University
Department of Food and Nutrition
College of Human Development and Education
Box 5057
Fargo, ND 58105-5057
ndsu.edu

Ohio

University of Akron
School of Family and Consumer Sciences
215 Schrank Hall South
Akron, OH 44325-6103
uakron.edu

Ohio University
School of Human and Consumer Sciences
101A Tupper Hall
Athens, OH 45701-2979
ohiou.edu

Bluffton College
Family and Consumer Sciences
280 W. College Ave.
Box 896
Bluffton, OH 45817-1196
ohwy.com/oh/b/bluffcol.htm

Bowling Green State University
Department of Family and Consumer Sciences
206 Johnston Hall
Bowling Green, OH 43403-0254
bgsu.edu

University of Cincinnati
Program in Dietetics and Nutrition Education
504 Dyer Hall, P.O. 210022
Cincinnati, OH 45221-0022
uc.edu

Case Western Reserve University
Department of Nutrition
10900 Euclid Ave.
Cleveland, OH 44106-4906
cwru.edu

Ohio State University
Department of Human Nutrition and Food Management
1787 Neil Ave.
Columbus, OH 43210-1295
osu.edu

University of Dayton
Health and Sports Science Department
Food and Nutrition Program
300 College Park
Dayton, OH 45469-1210
udayton.edu

Kent State University
School of Family and Consumer Studies
Nutrition and Dietetics Program
Nixson Hall
Kent, OH 44242-0001
kent.edu

Miami University
Department of Physical Education, Health, and Sport Studies
18 Phillips Hall
Oxford, OH 45056
miami.muohio.edu

Notre Dame College
4545 College Rd.
South Euclid, OH 44121-4293
ndc.edu

Youngstown State University
Human Ecology Department
One University Plaza
Youngstown, OH 44555-0001
ysu.edu

Oklahoma

University of Central Oklahoma
College of Education
Department of Human Environmental Sciences
Edmond, OK 73034-5209
ucok.edu

Langston University
Department of Human Ecology
308/304 Jones Hall
Langston, OK 73050
lunet.edu

University of Oklahoma Health Sciences Center
College of Allied Health
Department of Nutritional Sciences
P.O. Box 26901
Oklahoma City, OK 73190
ouhsc.edu

Oklahoma State University
Nutritional Sciences Department
HES 425
Stillwater, OK 74078-6141
okstate.edu

Northeastern State University
College of Business and Industry
Tahlequah, OK 74464-2399
nsuok.edu

Oregon

Oregon State University
Nutrition and Food Management Dietetic Program
14B Milam Hall
Corvallis, OR 97331-5103
orst.edu

Pennsylvania

Cedar Crest College
100 College Dr.
Allentown, PA 18104-6196
cedarcrest.edu

Messiah College
Department of Natural Sciences
Grantham, PA 17027
messiah.edu

Immaculata College
Department of Fashion-Foods and Nutrition
Box 722, 1145 King Rd.
Immaculata, PA 19345-0722
immaculata.edu

Indiana University of Pennsylvania
Department of Food and Nutrition
10 Ackerman Hall
Indiana, PA 15705-1087
iup.edu

Mansfield University
Simon B. Elliott Hall
Department of Health Sciences
Mansfield, PA 16933
mnsfld.edu

Drexel University
Nutrition and Food Sciences
Thirty-Second and Chestnut Sts.
Philadelphia, PA 19104-2875
drexel.edu

University of Pittsburgh
School of Health and Rehabilitation Sciences
Forbes Tower, Rm. 4052
Pittsburgh, PA 15260
pitt.edu

Marywood University
Department of Nutrition and Dietetics
2300 Adams Ave.
Scranton, PA 18509-1598
marywood.edu

Pennsylvania State University
Nutrition Department
College of Health and Human Development
University Park, PA 16802-6500
psu.edu

West Chester University
H302, Department of Health
Sturzebecker Health Sciences Center
West Chester, PA 19383
wcupa.edu

Puerto Rico

University of Puerto Rico
School of Home Economics
Box 23347, UPR Station
Rio Piedras Campus
San Juan, PR 00931-3347
upr.clu.edu

Rhode Island

University of Rhode Island
Department of Food Science and Nutrition
17 Woodward Hall
Kingston, RI 02881-0804
uri.edu

South Carolina

Clemson University
Department of Food Science
223 Poole Agricultural Center
Clemson, SC 29634-0371
clemson.edu

South Carolina State University
Department of Family and Consumer Sciences
Staley Hall, P.O. Box 7084
300 College Ave.
Orangeburg, SC 29117-0001
scsu.edu

Winthrop University
Department of Human Nutrition
Rock Hill, SC 29733
winthrop.edu

South Dakota

South Dakota State University
College of Family and Consumer Sciences
Department Nutrition and Food Science
P.O. Box 2275A
Brookings, SD 57007-0497
sdstate.edu

Mount Marty College
Department of N.F.S.
1105 W. Eighth St.
Yankton, SD 57078-3724
mtmc.edu

Tennessee

University of Tennessee at Chattanooga
Department of Human Ecology
202 Hunter Hall
Chattanooga, TN 37403-2598
utc.edu

Tennessee Technological University
School of Home Economics
Box 5035
Cookeville, TN 38505
tntech.edu

Carson-Newman College
Division of Family and Consumer Sciences
Box 71881
Jefferson City, TN 37760
cn.edu

East Tennessee State University
Department of Applied Human Sciences
P.O. Box 70671
Johnson City, TN 37614-0671
etsu.edu

University of Tennessee
College of Human Ecology
Department of Nutrition, Rm. 229
1215 Cumberland Ave.
Knoxville, TN 37996-1900
utk.edu

University of Tennessee at Martin
Department of Human Environmental Sciences
Gooch Hall, Rm. 340
Martin, TN 38238-5045
utm.edu

University of Memphis
Department of Consumer Science and Education
Memphis, TN 38152
memphis.edu

Middle Tennessee State University
Department of Human Sciences
Box 86
Murfreesboro, TN 37132
mtsu.edu

David Lipscomb University
Department of Family and Consumer Sciences
3901 Granny White Pike
Nashville, TN 37204-3951
lipscomb.edu

Tennessee State University
Department of Family and Consumer Sciences
P.O. Box 9598
3500 John A. Merritt Blvd.
Nashville, TN 37209-1561
tnstate.edu

Texas

Abilene Christian University
Department of Family and Consumer Sciences
ACU, Box 28155
Abilene, TX 79699
acu.edu

University of Texas, Austin
Department of Human Ecology
GEA 117
Austin, TX 78712-1097
utexas.edu

Lamar University
Department of Family and Consumer Sciences
Box 10035
Beaumont, TX 77710
lamar.edu

Texas A&M University
Human Nutrition Section
Department of Animal Science
College Station, TX 77843-2471
tamu.edu

Texas Woman's University
Department of Nutrition and Food Sciences
TWU Station 425888
Denton, TX 76204-5888
twu.edu

Texas Christian University
Department of Nutrition and Dietetics
Box 298600
Fort Worth, TX 76129
tcu.edu

Texas Southern University
Department of Human Sciences and Consumer Sciences
3100 Cleburne Ave.
Houston, TX 77004
tsu.edu

University of Houston
Department of Human Development and Consumer Sciences
4800 Calhoun Rd.
Houston, TX 77204-6861
uh.edu

Sam Houston State University
Food Science and Nutrition
Huntsville, TX 77341-2177
shsu.edu

Texas A&M University, Kingsville
Department of Human Sciences
Campus Box 168
Kingsville, TX 78363
tamuk.edu

Texas Tech University
Department of Education, Nutrition, and Restaurant, Hotel
    Management
Box 41162
Lubbock, TX 79409-1162
texastech.edu

Stephen F. Austin State University
Department of Human Sciences
P.O. Box 13014, SFA Station
Nacogdoches, TX 75962-3014
sfasu.edu

Prairie View A&M University
Department of Human Sciences
P.O. Box 4329
Prairie View, TX 77446-4329
pvamu.edu

University of Incarnate Word
4301 Broadway
San Antonio, TX 78209
uiw.edu

Southwest Texas State University
Family and Consumer Sciences
San Marcos, TX 78666-4616
txstate.edu

Tarleton State University
Department of Human Sciences
Box T-0380
Stephenville, TX 76402
tarleton.edu

Baylor University
Department of Family and Consumer Sciences
BU Box 97346
Waco, TX 76798-7346
baylor.edu

Utah

Brigham Young University
Food Science and Nutrition Department
S219 ESC
P.O. Box 24620
Provo, UT 84602-4620
byu.edu

Vermont

University of Vermont
Department of Nutritional Sciences
Terrill Hall
Burlington, VT 05405-0148
uvm.edu

Virginia

Virginia Polytechnic Institute & State University
Department of Human Nutrition, Foods, and Exercise
College of Human Resources and Education
Blacksburg, VA 24061-0430
vt.edu

James Madison University
Department of Dietetics/Health Sciences
MSC 1202, Moody Hall 213A
Harrisonburg, VA 22807
jmu.edu

Norfolk State University
Food Science and Nutrition/Chemistry
2401 Corprew Ave.
Norfolk, VA 23504-3992
nsu.edu

Virginia State University
Department of Human Ecology
Box 9211
Petersburg, VA 23806
vsu.edu

Radford University
Foods and Nutrition
P.O. Box 6962
Radford, VA 24142
runet.edu

Washington

Bastyr University
14500 Juanita Dr. NE
Bothell, WA 98011-4995
bastyr.edu

Central Washington University
Department of Family and Consumer Sciences
Ellensburg, WA 98926-7565
cwu.edu

Washington State University
College of Agriculture and Home Economics
Department of Food Science and Human Nutrition
Pullman, WA 99164-6376
wsu.edu

Seattle Pacific University
Department of Family and Consumer Sciences
3307 Third Ave. West
Seattle, WA 98119
spu.edu

University of Washington
305 Raitt Hall, Box 353410
Seattle, WA 98195-3410
washington.edu

West Virginia

West Virginia Wesleyan College
Department of Human Ecology
Haymond Hall 215E, Box 15
Buckhannon, WV 26201-2995
wwwc.edu

Marshall University
Family and Consumer Sciences
Huntington, WV 25755-2460
marshall.edu

West Virginia University
Division of Family Resources
College of Agriculture and Forestry
Allen Hall, Box 6124
Morgantown, WV 26506-6122
wvu.edu

Wisconsin

University of Wisconsin, Green Bay
Department of Human Biology
2420 Nicolet Dr.
Green Bay, WI 54311-7001
uwgb.edu

University of Wisconsin, Madison
Department of Nutritional Sciences
1415 Linden Dr.
Madison, WI 53706-1571
wisc.edu

University of Wisconsin, Stout
Dietetics Program
College of Human Development
Menomonie, WI 54751-0790
uwstout.edu

University of Wisconsin, Stevens Point
School of Health Promotion and Human Development
Stevens Point, WI 54481-3897
uwsp.edu

Wyoming

University of Wyoming
Department of Family and Consumer Sciences
Laramie, WY 82071-3354
uwyo.edu

For more information, access the American Dietetic Association at http://eatright.org.

For information on accredited undergraduate programs in dietetic education in Canada, go to: http://dietitians.ca.

Appendix C

Coordinated Undergraduate Programs

THE COORDINATED PROGRAM provides for the integration of academic course work with a minimum of nine hundred hours of supervised practice within a program granting at least a bachelor's degree.

Each program is accredited by the Commission on Accreditation/Approval for Dietetics Education and meets the minimum academic and supervised practice requirements established to be eligible for the registration examination for dietitians.

Following is a list of the currently accredited coordinated programs.

Alabama

University of Alabama
Department of Human Nutrition and Hospitality Management
P.O. Box 870158
Tuscaloosa, AL 35487-0158
ua.edu

California

Loma Linda University
School of Allied Health Professions
Department of Nutrition and Dietetics
Loma Linda, CA 92350
llu.edu

California State University, Los Angeles
Department of Health and Nutritional Sciences
5151 State University Dr.
Los Angeles, CA 90032-8172
calstatela.edu

Charles R. Drew University of Medicine and Science
College of Allied Health
1731 E. 120th St.
Los Angeles, CA 90059
cdrewu.edu

Connecticut

The University of Connecticut
School of Allied Health
358 Mansfield Rd., U-101
Storrs, CT 06269-2101
uconn.edu

Saint Joseph College
Department of Nutrition and Family Studies
1678 Asylum Ave.
West Hartford, CT 06117
sjc.edu

District of Columbia

Howard University
Department of Nutritional Sciences
Division of Allied Health Sciences
Sixth and Bryant Sts. NW, Annex I
Washington, DC 20059
howard.edu

Florida

Florida International University
Department of Dietetics and Nutrition
Health Bldg., Rm. 201
University Park
Miami, FL 33199
fiu.edu

Idaho

University of Idaho
School of Family and Consumer Sciences
College of Agriculture
Moscow, ID 83844-3183
uidaho.edu

Illinois

University of Illinois at Chicago
Department of Human Nutrition and Dietetics (M/C 517)
1919 W. Taylor St.
Chicago, IL 60612-7256
uic.edu

Indiana

Marian College
Department of Nursing and Nutrition Sciences
3200 Cold Spring Rd.
Indianapolis, IN 46222-1997
marian.edu

Indiana State University
Department of Family and Consumer Sciences
Terre Haute, IN 47809
indstate.edu

Purdue University
Department of Foods and Nutrition
1264 Stone Hall
West Lafayette, IN 47907-1264
purdue.edu

Kansas

Kansas State University
Department of Institution Management and Dietetics
Justin Hall 103
Manhattan, KS 66506-1404
ksu.edu

Kentucky

University of Kentucky
Nutrition and Food Science
204 Funkhouser
Lexington, KY 40506-0054
uky.edu

Massachusetts

Framingham State College
Department of Family and Consumer Sciences
100 State St.
Framingham, MA 01701-9101
framingham.edu

Michigan

Wayne State University
Department of Nutrition and Food Science
3009 Science Hall
Detroit, MI 48202
wayne.edu

Eastern Michigan University
Department of Human, Environmental, and Consumer Resources
206H Roosevelt Hall
Ypsilanti, MI 48197
emich.edu

Minnesota

College of St. Benedict/St. John's University
Nutrition Department
154 Ardolf Science Center
37 S. College Ave.
St. Joseph, MN 56374-2099
csbsju.edu

University of Minnesota
269 Food Science and Nutrition
1334 Eckles Ave.
St. Paul, MN 55108-6099
umn.edu

Mississippi

University of Southern Mississippi
Nutrition and Dietetics, College of Health-Human Sciences
Box 5035
Hattiesburg, MS 39406-5035
usm.edu

Missouri

University of Missouri, Columbia
Dietetic Education
318 Clark Hall
Columbia, MO 65211
missouri.edu

New Jersey

University of Medicine and Dentistry of New Jersey
School of Health Related Professions
65 Bergen St.
Newark, NJ 07107-3001
umdnj.edu

New York

D'Youville College
320 Porter Ave.
Buffalo, NY 14201-1084
dyc.edu

State University College, Buffalo
Nutrition, Hospitality, and Fashion Department
1300 Elmwood Ave.
Buffalo, NY 14222-1095
buffalo.edu

Rochester Institute of Technology
School of Food, Hotel, and Travel Management
George Eastman Bldg.
14 Lomb Memorial Dr.
Rochester, NY 14623-5604
rit.edu

Syracuse University
Department of Nutrition and Food-Service Management
034 Slocum Hall
Syracuse, NY 13244-1250
syr.edu

North Carolina

University of North Carolina
McGavran-Greenberg Hall
Department of Nutrition
CB #7400
Chapel Hill, NC 27599-7400
unc.edu

North Dakota

North Dakota State University
Department of Food and Nutrition
EML Hall 351
Fargo, ND 58105-5057
ndsu.edu

University of North Dakota
Department of Nutrition and Dietetics
Box 8237, University Station
Grand Forks, ND 58202-8237
und.nodak.edu

Ohio

The University of Akron
School of Home Economics and Family Ecology
215 Schrank Hall South
Akron, OH 44325-6103
uakron.edu

The Ohio State University
School of Allied Medical Professions
1583 Perry St.
Columbus, OH 43210-1234
osu.edu

Youngstown State University
One University Plaza
Youngstown, OH 44555-0001
ysu.edu

Oklahoma

University of Oklahoma Health Sciences Center
Department of Nutritional Sciences
Coordinated Program in Clinical Dietetics
P.O. Box 26901
Oklahoma City, OK 73190
ouhsc.edu

Pennsylvania

Edinboro University of Pennsylvania
Department of Biology and Health Services
Edinboro, PA 16444
edinboro.edu

Gannon University
College of Sciences, Engineering, and Health Sciences
109 University Square
Erie, PA 16541-0001
gannon.edu

Mercyhurst College
Department of Human Ecology
501 E. Thirty-Eighth St.
Erie, PA 16546-0001
mercyhurst.edu

Seton Hill College
Division of Management, Family, and Consumer Sciences
Greensburg, PA 15601-1599
setonhill.edu

University of Pittsburgh
School of Health and Rehabilitation Sciences
Forbes Tower, Rm. 4052
Pittsburgh, PA 15260
pitt.edu

Marywood University
Department of Nutrition and Dietetics
2300 Adams Ave.
Scranton, PA 18509-1598
marywood.edu

Texas

The University of Texas, Austin
Department of Human Ecology, A2700
Austin, TX 78712-1097
utexas.edu

The University of Texas Southwestern Medical Center
Southwestern Allied Health Sciences School
Department of Clinical Nutrition
5323 Harry Hines Blvd.
Dallas, TX 75235-8877
swmed.edu

The University of Texas-Pan American
College of Health Sciences and Human Services
1201 W. University Dr.
Edinburg, TX 78539-2999
panam.edu

Texas Christian University
Department of Nutrition and Dietetics
TCU Box 298600
Forth Worth, TX 76129
tcu.edu

Utah

Utah State University
Department of Nutrition and Food Sciences
Logan, UT 84322-8700
usu.edu

University of Utah
College of Health, Division of Foods and Nutrition
239N-HPER
Salt Lake City, UT 84112
utah.edu

Washington

Washington State University
FSHN Bldg., 106F
P.O. Box 646376
Pullman, WA 99164-6376
wsu.edu

Wisconsin

Viterbo College
Nutrition and Dietetics Department
815 S. Ninth St.
LaCrosse, WI 54601-4797
viterbo.edu

University of Wisconsin, Madison
Department of Nutritional Sciences
1415 Linden Dr.
Madison, WI 53706-1571
wisc.edu

Mount Mary College
Department of Dietetics
2900 N. Menomonee River Pkwy.
Milwaukee, WI 53222-4597
mtmary.edu

For more information, access the American Dietetic Association at http://eatright.org.

For information regarding coordinated undergraduate programs in Canada, go to http://dietitians.ca.

Appendix D

Dietetic Technician Programs

THE FOLLOWING PROGRAMS combine course work with supervised practice. However, these programs require fewer hours of supervised practice; graduates of these programs will have earned at least an associate's degree.

Following is a list of accredited/approved dietetic technician programs. Contact the school of your choice for further information or an enrollment application.

Arizona

Central Arizona College
8470 N. Overfield Rd.
Coolidge, AZ 85228
cac.cc.az.us

Arkansas

Black River Technical College
P.O. Box 468
Pocahontas, AR 72455
blackrivertech.edu

California

Orange Coast College
2701 Fairview Rd.
Costa Mesa, CA 92628-0120
occ.cccd.edu

Grossmont College
8800 Grossmont College Dr.
El Cajon, CA 92020-1799
grossmont.edu

Loma Linda University
Department of Nutrition & Dietetics
School of Allied Health Professions
Loma Linda, CA 92350
llu.edu

Long Beach City College
Liberal Arts Campus
Family and Consumer Studies Division
4901 E. Carson St.
Long Beach, CA 90808
lbcc.cc.ca.us

Los Angeles City College
Family and Consumer Studies
855 N. Vermont Ave.
Los Angeles, CA 90029-3590
lacitycollege.edu

Chaffey College
Food Service Management
5885 Haven Ave.
Rancho Cucamonga, CA 91737-3002
chaffey.edu

San Bernardino Valley College
Family and Consumer Science
701 S. Mount Vernon
San Bernardino, CA 92410
valleycollege.edu

Colorado

Front Range Community College
3645 W. 112th Ave.
Westminster, CO 80030
frcc.cc.co.us

Connecticut

Gateway Community Technical College
88 Bassett Rd.
North Haven, CT 06473
gateway.tec.wi.us

Briarwood College
2279 Mount Vernon Rd.
Southington, CT 06489
briarwood.edu

Florida

Florida Community College at Jacksonville, North Campus
4501 Capper Rd.
Jacksonville, FL 32218
fccj.org

Palm Beach Community College
Dietetic Technician Program
4200 Congress Ave.
Mail Station 32
Lake Worth, FL 33461-4796
pbcc.edu

Miami-Dade Community College
Mitchell Wolfson
300 NE Second Ave.
Miami, FL 33132-2297
mdc.edu

Pensacola Junior College
1000 College Blvd.
Pensacola, FL 32504-8998
pjc.cc.fl.us

Illinois

Malcolm X College
1900 W. Van Buren
Chicago, IL 60612-3145
ccc.edu/malcolmx

William Rainey Harper College
1200 W. Algonquin Rd.
Palatine, IL 60067-7398

Indiana

Purdue University-Calumet
Behavioral Sciences Department
2200 169th St.
Hammond, IN 46323-2094
calumet.purdue.edu

Ball State University
Department of Family and Consumer Sciences
150 Applied Technology
Muncie, IN 47306
bsu.edu

Louisiana

Delgado Community College
450 S. Claiborne Ave.
New Orleans, LA 70112-1310
dcc.edu

Maine

Southern Maine Technical College
Fort Rd.
South Portland, ME 04106

Maryland

Baltimore City Community College
Department of Allied Health
2901 Liberty Heights Ave.
Baltimore, MD 21215-7893
bccc.edu

Massachusetts

Laboure College
2120 Dorchester Ave.
Boston, MA 02124-5698
labourecollege.org

Essex Agricultural and Technical Institute
562 Maple St.
Hathorne, MA 01937
agtech.org

Michigan

Wayne County Community College
Dietetic Technology Program
8551 Greenfield Rd.
Detroit, MI 48228
wcccd.edu

Minnesota

Normandale Community College
9700 France Ave. South
Bloomington, MN 55431
normandale.edu

University of Minnesota, Crookston
Management Division
2900 University Ave.
Crookston, MN 56716-5001
crk.umn.edu

Missouri

St. Louis Community College at Florissant Valley
3400 Pershall Rd.
St. Louis, MO 63135-1499
stlcc.cc.mo.us

Nebraska

Southeast Community College
8800 "O" St.
Lincoln, NE 68520-1227
secc.kctcs.edu

Nebraska Methodist College
Metropolitan Community Consortium
8501 W. Dodge Rd.
Omaha, NE 68114
methodistcollege.edu

New Hampshire

University of New Hampshire
Thompson School of Applied Science
Cole Hall
Durham, NH 03824
unh.edu

New Jersey

Camden County College
P.O. Box 200
Blackwood, NJ 08012
camdencc.edu

Middlesex County College
2600 Woodbridge Ave.
P.O. Box 3050
Edison, NJ 08818-3050
middlesex.cc.nj.us

New York

Genesee Community College
One College Rd.
Batavia, NY 14020-9704
genesee.edu

LaGuardia Community College
City University of New York
31-10 Thomson Ave.
Long Island City, NY 11101
lagcc.cuny.edu

State University of New York
Agriculture and Technical College
Bailey Annex
Morrisville, NY 13408
suny.edu

Dutchess Community College
53 Pendell Rd.
Poughkeepsie, NY 12601-1595
sunydutchess.edu

Suffolk County Community College
Eastern Campus
121 Speonk-Riverhead Rd.
Riverhead, NY 11901-3499
sunysuffolk.edu

Rockland Community College
145 College Rd.
Suffern, NY 10901-3699
sunyrockland.edu

Westchester Community College
75 Grasslands Rd.
Valhalla, NY 10595-1698
sunywcc.edu

Erie Community College
North Campus
6205 Main St.
Williamsville, NY 14221-7095
ecc.edu

Ohio

Cincinnati State Technical and Community College
Health Technologies Division
3520 Central Pkwy.
Cincinnati, OH 45223-2690

Cuyahoga Community College
2900 Community College Ave.
Cleveland, OH 44115
tri-c.cc.oh.us

Columbus State Community College
550 E. Spring St.
P.O. Box 1609
Columbus, OH 43216-1609
cscc.edu

Sinclair Community College
444 W. Third St.
Dayton, OH 45402-1460
sinclair.edu

Lima Technical College
4240 Campus Dr.
Lima, OH 45804-3597

Hocking Technical College
3301 Hocking Pkwy.
Nelsonville, OH 45764-9704
hocking.edu

Owens Community College
P.O. Box 10000
Toledo, OH 43699-1947
owens.cc.oh.us

Youngstown State University
Department of Human Ecology
One University Plaza
Cushwa Hall, Rm. 3048
Youngstown, OH 44555-3344
ysu.edu

Muskingum Area Technical College
Division Health, Public Services and General Studies
1555 Newark Rd.
Zanesville, OH 43701
oache.org/cd/muskingum.htm

Oklahoma

Oklahoma State University, Okmulgee
1801 E. Fourth St.
Okmulgee, OK 74447-3901
osu-okmulgee.edu

Oregon

Portland Community College
12000 SW Forty-Ninth
P.O. Box 19000
Portland, OR 97280-0990
pcc.edu

Pennsylvania

Community College of Philadelphia
1700 Spring Garden St.
Philadelphia, PA 19130-3991
ccp.edu

Community College of Allegheny County
Allegheny Campus
808 Ridge Ave.
Pittsburgh, PA 15212-6097
ccac.edu

The Pennsylvania State University
College of Health and Human Development
School of Hotel, Restaurant, and Recreation Management
University Park, PA 16802-1307
psu.edu

Westmoreland County Community College
Commissioners Hall
Armbrust Rd.
Youngwood, PA 15697-1895
wccc-pa.edu

South Carolina

Greenville Technical College
ET13A
P.O. Box 5616
Greenville, SC 29606-5616
greenvilletech.com

Tennessee

Shelby State Community College
P.O. Box 40568
Memphis, TN 38174-0568

Texas

Tarrant County Junior College
2100 TCJC Pkwy.
Arlington, TX 76018
tcjc.cc.tx.us

El Paso Community College
100 W. Rio Grande Ave.
El Paso, TX 79902
epcc.edu

San Jacinto College Central
8060 Spencer Hwy.
P.O. Box 2007
Pasadena, TX 77501-2007
sjcd.cc.tx.us

St. Philip's College
1801 Martin Luther King
San Antonio, TX 78203-2098
accd.edu/spc/spcmain/spc.htm

Virginia

Northern Virginia Community College
HRI/DIT McDiarmid Bldg.
8333 Little River Turnpike
Annadale, VA 22003-3796
nv.cc.va.us

J. Sargeant Reynolds Community College
P.O. Box 85622
Richmond, VA 23285-5622
jsr.cc.va.us

Tidewater Community College
1700 College Crescent
Virginia Beach, VA 23456
tcc.edu

Washington

Shoreline Community College
16101 Greenwood Ave. North
Seattle, WA 98133
oscar.ctc.edu/shoreline

Spokane Community College
North 1810 Greene St., MS 2090
Spokane, WA 99207-5399
ol.scc.spokane.edu

Wisconsin

Madison Area Technical College
3550 Anderson St.
Madison, WI 53704-2599
matcmadison.edu/matc

Milwaukee Area Technical College
West Campus
1200 S. Seventy-First St.
West Allis, WI 52314-3110
matc.edu

For more information, access the American Dietetic Association at http://eatright.org.

Appendix E

Pre-Professional Practice Programs (AP4)

The pre-professional practice program provides a minimum of nine hundred hours of supervised practice. Programs follow completion of at least a bachelor's degree and course work requirements. Programs are usually completed in nine to twenty-four months, depending on the availability of a part-time schedule or requirement of graduate credit.

Listed below are the currently approved pre-professional practice programs.

Alabama

Oakwood College
Family and Consumer Sciences
Oakwood Rd.
Huntsville, AL 35896
oakwood.edu

Alaska

University of Alaska, Anchorage
3211 Providence Dr.
Anchorage, AK 99508-8357
uaa.alaska.edu

Arizona

Focus on Nutrition
3923 E. Thunderbird Rd., Ste. 26-113
Phoenix, AZ 85032
azdpac.org/focus.htm

Paradise Valley Unified School District
20621 N. Thirty-Second St.
Phoenix, AZ 85024
pvusd.k12.az.us

Walter O. Boswell Memorial Hospital
10401 W. Thunderbird Blvd.
Sun City, AZ 85372
sunhealth.net/boswell

Arizona State University
Department of Family Resources and Human Development
Box 872502
Tempe, AZ 85287-2502
asu.edu

Maricopa County
Department of Public Health
Office of Nutrition Services-AP4
1414 W. Broadway, Ste. 237
Tempe, AZ 85282
maricopa.gov/public_health

California

University of California, Berkeley
Department of Nutritional Sciences
119 Morgan Hall
Berkeley, CA 94720-3104
berkeley.edu

ARAMARK Healthcare Support Services
2600 Michelson, Ste. 1170
Irvine, CA 92612
aramark.ca

Connecticut

Danbury Hospital
24 Hospital Ave.
Danbury, CT 06810
danhosp.org

Florida

The University of North Florida
College of Health
Department of Health Science
4567 St. Johns Bluff Rd. South
Jacksonville, FL 32224
unf.edu

Georgia

University of Georgia
Department of Foods and Nutrition
Dawson Hall
Athens, GA 30602-3622
uga.edu

Indiana

Purdue University Calumet
Department of Behavioral Sciences
2200 169th St.
Hammond, IN 46323-2094
calumet.purdue.edu

Kentucky

Morehead State University
Department of Home Economics
P.O. Box 889
Morehead, KY 40351-1689
morehead-st.edu

Maryland

University of Maryland Eastern Shore
Department of Human Ecology
Princess Anne, MD 21853
umes.edu

Massachusetts

Sodexho Marriott Services
153 Second Ave.
Waltham, MA 02454
sodexho-usa.com

Michigan

University of Michigan Hospitals
C333 MedInn Bldg., Box 0832
1500 E. Medical Center Dr.
Ann Arbor, MI 48109-0832
med.umich.edu

Andrews University
Department of Nutrition
Berrien Springs, MI 49104-0210
andrews.edu

New Jersey

Montclair State University
Department of Human Ecology
Upper Montclair, NJ 07043
montclair.edu

New York

Lehman College
The City University of New York
Department of Health Services
Bedford Park Blvd. West
Bronx, NY 10468-1539
lehman.cuny.edu

Brooklyn College
Department of Health and Nutrition Sciences
2900 Bedford Ave.
Brooklyn, NY 11210-2889
brooklyn.cuny.edu

The Long Island College Hospital
Nutrition and Food-Service Department
Atlantic Ave. and Hicks St.
Brooklyn, NY 11201

Sodexho Marriott Services-Metropolitan
New York AP4 Program
90 Merrick Ave., Ste. 210
East Meadow, NY 11554
sodexho-usa.com

Golden Hill Health Care Center
99 Golden Hill Dr.
Kingston, NY 12401-6442
co.ulster.ny.us/goldenhill

ARAMARK Healthcare Support Services
Metropolitan New York, AP4
aramark.ca

Hunter College
Nutrition and Food Science Program
School of Health Sciences
425 E. Twenty-Fifth St.
New York, NY 10010-2590
hunter.cuny.edu

Mount Sinai Medical Center
One Gustave L. Levy Pl.
Box 1066
New York, NY 10029
mountsinai.org

Pennsylvania

The Wood Company
6081 Hamilton Blvd.
P.O. Box 3501
Allentown, PA 18106-0501
duf.net/aliresume.htm

South Dakota

South Dakota University Affiliated Program
The University of South Dakota School of Medicine
414 E. Clark St.
Vermillion, SD 57069-2390
usd.edu/med

Texas

Lamar University
Department of Family and Consumer Sciences
P.O. Box 10035
Beaumont, TX 77710
cob.lamar.edu

Stephen F. Austin State University
SFA Station 13014
Nacogdoches, TX 75962-3014
sfasu.edu

Wisconsin

University of Wisconsin Hospital and Clinics
Food and Nutrition Services, F4/120
600 Highland Ave.
Madison, WI 53792
wisc.edu

For more information, access the American Dietetic Association at
http://eatright.org.

Notes

Chapter 1

1. Chappa, Stacey. "Boomer Ready Initiative: Identification of Wellness Needs." *J. Am. Diet. Assoc.* 6:878, 2004.
2. Peregrin, Tony. "Career Advancement: Tips for Success While on the Job Hunt." *J. Am. Diet. Assoc.* 8:1215, 2004.

Chapter 2

1. Tumer, C. E. "Health Education as a World Movement." *J. Am. Diet. Assoc.* 12:457, 1936.
2. American Dietetic Association. "Key Trends Affecting the Dietetics Profession and the American Dietetic Association." *J. Am. Diet. Assoc.* December, 2002.

Chapter 4

1. The American Dietetic Association. "Position Paper on Nutrition Services in Health Maintenance Organizations." *J. Am. Diet. Assoc.*

Chapter 5

1. Baldwin, Cheryl J. "Food and Fitness Careers for Dietitians." *J. Am. Diet. Assoc.* November, 2002.
2. Hunt, Alice, Kathryn Hilgenkamp, and Richard Farley. "Skills and Competencies of Dietitians Practicing in Wellness Settings." *J. Am. Diet. Assoc.* December, 2000.
3. "2002 Dietetics Compensation & Benefits Survey." Chicago: American Dietetic Association, 2003.
4. Goldberg, Jeanne P., and Jennifer P. Hellig. "Nutrition Communication: Exciting Opportunities for Dietitians." *J. Am. Diet. Assoc.* January, 2003.

Chapter 6

1. Wagstaff, M., and M. Mattfeldt-Beman. "The Fitness Opportunity for Dietetic Educators and Practitioners." *J. Am. Diet. Assoc.* 84:1465, 1984.
2. *Webster's Tenth New Collegiate Dictionary*, 1996, p. 930.
3. Ibid.
4. Hager, Mary H. "Medicare Reform Opens Door for Preventive Nutrition Services." *J. Am. Diet. Assoc.* 6:887, 2004.

Chapter 8

1. "2002 Dietetics Compensation & Benefits Survey." Chicago: American Dietetic Association, 2003.
2. Pinkley, Robin L. "Salary and Compensation Negotiation Skills for Young Professionals." *J. Am. Diet. Assoc.* 7:1064, 2004.

Chapter 10

1. American Dietetic Association, 1998–99 (http://eatright.org).
2. Cotugna, Nancy, Connie E. Vickey. "Perceptions and Evaluation of the Computerized Examination for Dietitians." *J. Am. Diet. Assoc.* December, 2001.
3. Ivens, Barbara J. "Recognizing the Dietetics Profession." *J. Am. Diet. Assoc.* February, 2004.

Chapter 11

1. American Dietetic Association. "Key Trends Affecting the Dietetics Profession and the ADA." *J. Am. Diet. Assoc.* December, 2002.
2. Moen, Ronald S., and Marsha Sharp. "International Dietetics." *J. Am. Diet. Assoc.* January, 2004.

About the Author

CAROL COLES CALDWELL is a graduate of the University of Arizona in Tucson, where she received her bachelor's degree in 1980 and master's in 1981, both in nutritional sciences. In 1986, she graduated from the New York Cooking School, where she developed a foundation in French cooking techniques. This enabled her to combine the disciplines of cooking and nutrition.

Starting in 1983, Ms. Caldwell managed the nutrition department at Canyon Ranch Spa Resort in Tucson, Arizona. She then went to Miami, Florida, in 1986 to develop the nutrition and food program for the Doral Saturnia Spa. Ms. Caldwell returned to New York City as a nutrition and food consultant in 1987. As a consultant, she has taught spa cuisine cooking classes at the New York Cooking School; developed nutritional software for Nutridata Software Corporation; advised Children's Television Workshop on the nutritive quality of proposed *Sesame Street* brand children's snack foods; developed healthy menus for restaurants; and catered nutritional cuisine for private parties in New York. In addition, Ms.

Caldwell has written articles for major magazines such as *New Woman*, *New Body*, and *Mademoiselle*. In 1993, she collaborated with the Culinary Institute of America to write *The Professional Chef's Techniques of Healthy Cooking*.

Ms. Caldwell worked as a consultant with Commercial Aluminum Cookware Company, the makers of Calphalon cookware. She developed recipes for use in promotions, cooking classes, and brochures. In addition, Ms. Caldwell created recipes for American Spoon Foods, a specialty food company located in Petoskey, Michigan.